C000264455

# ANIMAL LORE and LEGEND

RUTH BINNEY

# ANIMAL LORE and LEGEND

## THE WISDOM AND WONDER OF
## ANIMALS REVEALED

RP

**RYDON**
PUBLISHING

A Rydon Publishing Book
35 The Quadrant
Hassocks
West Sussex
BN6 8BP
www.rydonpublishing.co.uk
www.rydonpublishing.com

First published by Rydon Publishing in 2017

A CIP catalogue record for this book is available from the British Library.

ISBN: 978-1-910821-15-2

Printed in Poland by BZ Graf

# CONTENTS

# INTRODUCTION

**For as long as humans have inhabited the earth, we have lived alongside the mulititude of other creatures with which we share our planet. As they were establishing their first civilizations, humans must have quickly come to recognize which of their fellow creatures were harmful and dangerous, and which were useful – whether as home guards, means of transport, or sources of food. It is not hard to imagine animals approaching the camp fires of early settlements, and the resulting human reactions towards them, or the terrors of being confronted by man-eating carnivores.**

The emotions that our fellow creatures invoke may well be benign – as exemplified by our relationships with the pets and domestic animals we cherish – or they may be a great deal more fearful or reverent. However it is undoubtedly true that today most of us are not as close to the animals around us as our forebears were, and that many of the world's best loved large mammals and most beautiful birds are in danger of becoming extinct. The threats of the 21st century to the animal world make it even more pertinent to explore the many legends and folktales, myths and superstitions that reflect this past closeness, highlight our desire to explain nature's wonders and mysteries, and underline the necessity to preserve for the benefit of future generations all creatures great and small.

Exploring the lore and legends of the animal world makes it abundantly clear that the characters of animals have become an integral part of our descriptive language. Owls are wise and lions are brave; bears are strong and monkeys mischievous; bees are busy and doves gentle. Yet whatever their natural attributes, in folklore animals can do almost anything. They can be our friends and foes – and of course they can talk to each other. They can be evil witches and devils in disguise, and the objects of hate and opprobrium. They can bring good luck and bad. And in real life they can be our dearest companions, to the point of sheer worship.

Animals can even help to heal our ills and have proved effective in treating mental illness. They have been used for centuries to help cure the diseases that once unmercifully wiped out adults and children, including plague, whooping cough and tuberculosis; they were also employed to ease the unbearable pain of toothache and gout. Not all of nature's fauna works for good, of course. Bees and wasps sting (although bee stings are said to cure rheumatism), while mosquitoes and fleas spread malaria and plague. Understanding the difference between 'kill' and 'cure', when embroidered with lore and legend, reveals some fascinating insights.

If we wish to predict the future by way of horoscopes and the like, then animals can also be involved. The animal symbols 'seen' in the sky in the form of constellations, and their changing positions relative to the sun and the planets, have for millennia been used to predict the fates of people born in different months of the year or, according to the Chinese zodiac, different years. Whether or not we believe astrologists' predictions, the animal symbolism itself remains enormously powerful.

As well as the realities of nature, delving into the fascinating world of 'invented' creatures, from mermaids to dragons and vampires, reveals yet more secrets of our long-standing relationship with animals and the myths that have grown up around them. In my younger days I once swam in the deep, pitch black waters of Loch Ness, trying to imagine whether I really was sharing space with the famous monster.

In the creation of this book many thanks are due to my editors Freya Dangerfield and Verity Graves-Morris, designer Prudence Rogers and to my publisher Robert Ertle. It is dedicated to animal lovers everywhere.

*Ruth Binney,*
*Yeovil, Somerset, 2017*

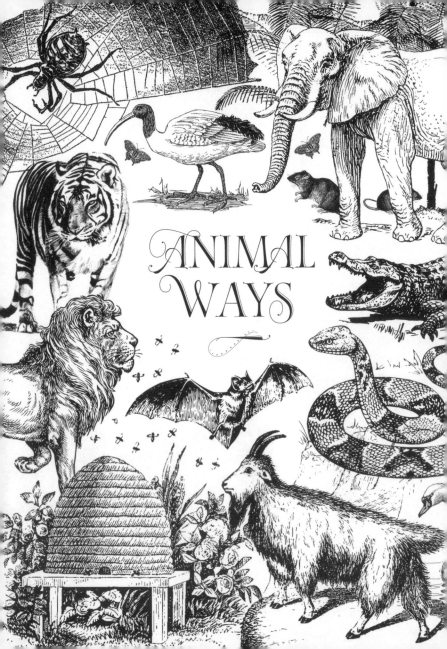

# ANIMAL WAYS

**F**rom bees to bats, from beetles to bears, and from salmon to swans, each of the many animals and birds in the world's fauna has its own individual character. So strongly imbued are the extraordinary 'personalities' and powers of many animals that the ancients, who were meticulous observers of the world around them, believed these creatures to be the embodiments of deities or to be closely linked with them.

In countless tales told down the ages – including the Bible and other religious texts – the powers of animals are colourfully recounted, often with some kind of moral attached. As a result it has become almost second nature for us to think of snakes as evil (although they can also be good), of rats as dirty, and of asses as stupid. Equally we revere the memories of elephants, the strength of lions and the cunning of foxes.

As a result of their typical behaviour, and the place that they have achieved in lore and legend the world over, certain animals have also become symbolic of all kinds of attributes. So the dove that brought the olive branch back to Noah's Ark is a bird of peace; the eagle, icon of the USA, is a bird of victory; and the swan is the symbol of pure beauty. These qualities have translated themselves into our language and iconography, and into literature and film. Indeed some of the world's most popular and enduring cartoon characters include the cat and mouse Tom and Jerry, Yogi Bear and the 101 Dalmations.

# Little birds that know

**Since ancient times birds, because of their keen eyesight and aerial view of the world, have been linked with wisdom and knowledge. Owls and ibises are believed to be especially wise.**

*A wise old owl sat in an oak,*
*The more he saw the less he spoke,*
*The less he spoke the more he heard,*
*Wasn't that owl a wise old bird?*

So runs the children's rhyme (which is as much a lesson in listening as on the good sense of the owl, and has the alternative last line 'Why can't we all be like that wise old bird?'). However the owl's association with knowledge stems largely from the fact that the bird was companion to Athene, Greek goddess of wisdom, sciences and the arts. So strong was the connection that Athenian coins bearing the head of the goddess on one side were marked on the other with an owl and an olive branch (symbol of peace and plenty) from the tree believed to have been given to the earth by Athene. However, there is no known link between the owl's symbolic wisdom and its naturally 'bespectacled' knowing looks.

**In the Christian tradition**, the owl is associated with St Jerome, who was described as the fountain of wisdom, a reputation earned from the fact that he was a translator of the Bible and the foremost biblical scholar of his day.

**IN THE DAYS** of King Arthur and his Knights of the Round Table, the owl was linked with the wizard Merlin, and customarily depicted on his shoulder. The 'real' Merlin was probably a Celtic bard.

In ancient Egypt the god Thoth, creator and commander of the universe, god of writing and knowledge, protector of scribes and keeper of the records of the dead, was commonly depicted with the body of a man and the head of an ibis, whose reputation for wisdom may have stemmed from its annual arrival in Egypt at the time of the Nile's inundation. Later, Thoth became linked with keepers of dangerous secrets and the occult.

# The cruel crocodile

**The crocodile is the embodiment of hypocrisy – the creature who 'smiles' at you, then gobbles you up. The alligator (early writing made no distinction between the two) is equally feared.**

The crocodile, described by a 16th-century explorer as 'cowardly on land, cruel in the water', was said to lure its prey with moaning sounds then, having devoured its meal,

**IT IS A WIDESPREAD** urban legend that alligators inhabit the sewers of New York. They are said to be adult versions of small, rejected pets bought in Florida and flushed down toilets.

to shed tears of false remorse. Its hypocritical habits are wonderfully evoked by Edmund Spenser in *The Faerie Queen*, in these lines depicting the meeting of 'a weary traveller' and his attacker:

*Which, in false griefe hyding his harmfull guile,*
*Doth weep full sore, and sheddeth tender teares:*
*The foolish man, that pitties all this while*
*His mournfull plight, is swallowed up unawares...*

## OUTWITTING THE CROCODILE

It takes the supreme cunning of a fox to foil a crocodile, as this South African folktale describes:

A big crocodile was killing sheep, cattle and people, and the king called a meeting to see how it might be banished. Fox jumped up and said: 'O King, I am small but wisdom surpasses bravery. Why do you wait for your enemy to grow strong? What do I do? I eat crocodiles while they are still in the eggs. Get rid of your enemy before he is stronger than you.'

Crocodiles do certainly make mournful noises, though their 'tears' are thought by zoologists to be the creature's natural mechanism for shedding excess salt rather than revealing their temperament. And not all who approach are attacked. After feeding, the Nile crocodile will lie with its huge mouth agape and allow small plovers or 'crocodile birds' to clean its mouth, teeth and throat.

# Cunning as the fox

**Everything about the fox's looks and behaviour portray an expert in cunning. This inveterate night hunter will trick its pursuers by tracking in circles and even by making friends with the dogs specifically trained to chase it down in the hunt.**

Farmer and fox have long had an uneasy relationship. As a plunderer of poultry the fox is a hated enemy, but he also catches the rabbits and other vermin that destroy crops. Its nature is contradictory – it is both destructive and creative, bold but timid, defensive yet at ease in almost any environment, from open fields to the city streets.

The fox figures widely in fables. In Aesop's story 'The Fox and the Crane' the two creatures are apparently on good terms. Fox invites the bird to share a meal, but for a joke serves soup in a flat dish. Fox laps it up with ease but Crane cannot eat. Crane then invites Fox to dine and serves soup in long-necked bottles, which only Crane, with his long bill, can reach. The moral of the tale is that turning the tables is fair play.

**Legends of** many lands relate that the vixen is a sorceress in disguise, lurking in the forests and sometimes assuming the looks of a beautiful woman who, once she had cast her evil spell, changes to animal form.

# Spider talents

**The 19th-century poem by Mary Howitt that begins '"Will you walk into my parlour?" said the spider to the fly' sums up the spider's cunning in luring its prey into its web. These creatures, feared by many to the point of phobia, get their name from the Old English word *spinnan*, a spinner.**

In West Africa, where it's said, 'The wisdom of the spider is greater than that of all the world put together', the supreme trickster is the spider Anansi. People also say: 'Woe to him who would put his trust in Anansi – a sly, selfish and greedy fellow.' One story relates how a farmer put a gum doll (a kind of sticky scarecrow) in a field to stop his crops being stolen.

**'EIGHT LEGS, two fangs and an attitude'** was the tagline of the 1990 movie *Arachnophobia*, in which a South American killer spider hitches a lift to the US in a coffin and starts to breed and kill.

Confronted with the doll, Anansi kicked him, but his feet and hands got stuck. Finding his thief, the farmer beat Anansi until his body was flat, and he had the mark of the cross on his back.

The arachnids, the zoological group to which spiders belong, are named from the spider's association with Arachne, a Greek girl who was renowned for her skill at spinning and weaving. When she dared to challenge the goddess Athene to a weaving contest, the tactless Arachne completed a wonderful depiction of the loves of the gods. Consumed with fury at her rival's skill, Athene changed Archne into a spider, condemning her to a life of eternal weaving.

**PRECIOUS CREATURES**

Protect spiders and their webs because:

- When Jesus was born in a manger, he was protected by a spider's web.
- Sweep a spider out of the door and you will sweep away your luck.
- Spiders and cobwebs in stables prevent horses from going lame.
- 'If in life you want to thrive,/Let a spider run alive'.
- A spider's web on a boat will prevent the craft from sinking.

# A complete turkey

**The bird that graces our dinner tables at Christmas and Thanksgiving is renowned for its lack of guile in allowing itself to be caught and eaten, as well as for its gobbling voice.**

The turkey was widely regarded as an interloper when it arrived in Europe from the Americas in the early 16th century and was said to have 'violated the rights of hospitality'. In a 19th-century drawing that expresses the unworthiness of this sentiment a turkey cock is shown, with plumes spread, meeting a proud cockerel, its spurs on its legs lifted ready to attack. Underneath is a verse from Leviticus: 'And if a stranger sojurn with thee in your land ye shall not vex him.'

In its native lands the turkey is thought by some to be a cowardly creature and certain tribes would, on this account, refuse to eat its meat lest they be similarly afflicted. As for its voice, one Cherokee Indian tale tells how the turkey, regretting its feeble tones, asked the grouse to teach it to call more loudly. The grouse accepted, but asked for payment in return. The turkey offered some feathers (which the grouse is said to wear round its neck to this day), but when the time came for the turkey to try out his improved voice he got so agitated that he could only let out a gobble.

**In the turkey trot**, an American folk dance, partners flap their arms at each other like turkey wings. 'Turkey in the Straw' is traditionally danced to the accompaniment of fiddles and banjos.

**THE SAYING** 'to talk turkey' means to discuss frankly – it is said to derive from the turkey's habit of revealing its presence to hunters making gobbling noises by gobbling in return.

# Safe with the dolphins

**The notion that dolphins can rescue people from drowning or guide them safely through the water goes back centuries. Today it is claimed that dolphin therapy may be a cure for mental ills.**

On a Mediterranean sea journey in the 7th century BC the Greek poet and harpist Arion was set upon by sailors who discovered that he was carrying gold – his prize for winning a musical competition. Before they threw him overboard, the sailors granted Arion's request to play one final melody. Attracted by the beauty of his music, a school of dolphins swam around the ship. Arion leapt into the sea and was carried to safety on a dolphin's back.

**THERAPISTS** have found that swimming with dolphins is an excellent remedy for depression.

Dolphins also attended the deities, notably the sea-god Poseidon, whose seashell chariot they pulled through the waters, and it was after Cretan sailors had been guided there by a dolphin sent by Apollo that the famous oracle was founded at Delphi.

If you should die at sea, dolphins may save your corpse from being eaten by the fishes. It is said that dolphins know by the smell of a dead man whether or not he has ever killed and eaten one of their kind. If they judge him not guilty, they will bring his body to shore, intact, for his relatives to find. In Christian legend, the body of Lucian of Antioch, martyred in 312 CE, was brought ashore by a dolphin after it had been thrown into the sea to deny the saint a Christian burial.

# The pure and gentle dove

**Especially when feathered in white – the colour of purity – the dove is the perfect symbol of the undefiled simplicity of the soul. Its special significance in the Judeo-Christian tradition comes from its many appearances in the Bible.**

It is the dove's gentle demeanour and quiet habits that have led to its symbolic association with the best behaviour, but most significantly it represents the Holy Spirit at Christ's baptism. St Luke's Gospel records: 'During a general baptism of the people, when Jesus had been baptized and was praying, heaven opened and the Holy Spirit descended on him in bodily form like a dove, and there came a voice from heaven, "You are my beloved Son; in you I delight".' The symbolic use of the bird on this occasion was no accident, since it had long been associated with the Jewish rite of purification.

## DOVE DEEDS AND LORE
- Doves get their scientific family name Columbidae from their association with St Columba, who had a vision of the Holy Spirit in the form of a dove.
- If you make three wishes when hearing the first dove in spring they will all come true.
- The dove lays only two eggs because she has pride in – and concern for – the family she will raise.
- The dead may be reincarnated as doves.

The dove was the bird that Noah sent out from the Ark to see if the flood had subsided. When it returned with 'an olive leaf plucked off' in its beak he knew that this was so. Ever since, the dove and olive branch have been symbols not only of peace and gentleness between God and humans but also between nations.

# The stupid ass

**The ass takes centre stage in stories that epitomize stupidity (although it does have redeeming features), but it was once also associated with evil. We are all, on occasion, likely to make asses of ourselves.**

To the Egyptians, an ass was an animal to be approached with care, and to meet a red ass (the colour of blood) was believed to be fatal to the soul, preventing it from attaining the hereafter. It was associated with Seth, the god of chaos and incarnation of evil, who murdered his brother, Osiris.

Of the 27 tales that Aesop tells about the ass, typical is 'The Ass Who Was Taken for a Lion': 'An ass, clothed in the skin of a lion, passed himself off in the eyes of everyone as a lion, and made everyone flee from him, both men and animals. But the wind came and blew off the lion's skin, leaving him naked and exposed. Everyone then fell upon him when they saw this, and beat him with sticks and clubs.' The moral is, be ordinary and poor: pretensions will make you an object of ridicule.

# The Devil's goat

When, in medieval times, Satan was believed to take on the form of an animal, the goat was most often cast in this evil role. Other vile associations come from the ritual of the scapegoat.

**The 13th-century monk** Matthew Paris told of a black billy goat, said to have been an evil spirit that carried the body of King William II (William Rufus) to judgement. The king, hated by his subjects for his cruelty, had been shot and killed by an arrow while out hunting in 1100.

The goat's evil reputation stems from accounts such as that of the trials in 1335 of Anne-Marie de Georgel and Catherine Delort from Toulouse, who were accused of having had sexual relations with the Devil in the form of a goat. And in 1460 the witches of Arras were condemned because they worshipped and made offerings to the Devil in similar guise. The trial record made special mention of the fact that 'with candles in their hands they kiss the hind parts of the goat that is the Devil'.

 **SHEEP GOOD,** goats bad: that is the Biblical assessment, by which they are destined to be separated at the Day of Judgement.

The concept of the scapegoat, an animal that takes on the sin of another, comes from an ancient Jewish ritual described in Leviticus. Two goats were taken to the altar of the tabernacle, where the high priest cast lots, earmarking one animal for Yaweh (the Lord) and the other for Azazel (the evil one). The Lord's goat was sacrificed, while the scapegoat, though spared, was doomed to take on the sins of the people and the priest. After the ceremony it was led away and allowed to escape into the wilderness, carrying the sins with it.

# Piggy tales

❧✿❧

**The unfortunate pig is often the butt of opprobium, having been associated over the centuries with the Devil and demons, and declared 'unclean'. By contrast, the porker's intelligence is celebrated in many countries.**

When God advised Noah which animals to take into the ark he distinguished between 'clean' and 'unclean' animals. The pig was declared unclean because it has cloven hooves but, unlike a cow, does not chew the cud. Small holes in the creatures' forefeet are believed to be the marks where the Devil's disciples entered them.

Like goats, pigs were also believed to be the Devil in disguise, or they might have been the incarnations of witches. In 1457 a pig was even tried and condemned to death, though her piglets were saved. The Yird (earth) Pig was believed to roam graveyards, feasting on corpses. The pig was also reviled for its behaviour, including gluttony and laziness.

**Many old English churches** are said to owe their siting to the founder being given helpful guidance by a pig. At Winwick in Lancashire, where a pig is carved on the church front, it is said that pigs even carried the stones for the church's construction in their mouths.

Yet in ancient Crete the pig was so highly esteemed that it became an object of worship. Pigs – usually small, suckling pigs – were sacrificed to Demeter, goddess of the earth and fertility, and eating the animal's meat, except as a sacrifice, was taboo. The ancient Celts also worshipped the pig, and considered pork to be the best of all meats.

Today, pigs are esteemed for their sense of smell and ability to find prized truffles. As such, pigs have rarely been as successful as in 1858 when the Marquis des Isnards witnessed the unearthing of a monster fungus weighing 25kg (55lb). However experts of today favour dogs for truffle hunting, not least because pigs have a tendency to consume the delicacies they unearth.

# Beware the bats

꽃

**Many features of bats conspire to underline their sinister reputation – not least their leathery wings, fluttering flight and their habit of roosting in caves, ruins and other dark, spooky places.**

Until its mammalian identity was clarified, the bat was a mystery. Known as a flitter-mouse or *avis, non avis*, meaning 'bird and not bird', in folklore it took a dual role, as both the symbol of the soul and the personification of the evil one who dwells in darkness. As the Devil in disguise, bats were hounded and killed from ancient times. Even in the 20th century they were sometimes nailed with outstretched wings to the doors of Sicilian homes to protect their occupants from disaster.

**BATS' BLOOD was regularly used by sorceresses in their black masses and by witches in their flying ointment.**

Bats could also, it was thought, be the embodiment of vampires – the living dead who fed on the blood of their human victims – or witches in animal form, which made it particularly unlucky to find a bat in the house or even flying around it. A bat circling a house three times was taken as a sign of impending death. And seeing bats ascending into the air, then flying straight down again, was said to indicate that witches were due to meet nearby. As an antidote to such danger, it was thought that protection could be achieved by carrying a bat bone.

To rid people of evil spirits it is a widespread practice to 'magic' out a bat, usually via the mouth. One story relates how a Frenchman suffering from melancholia was brought a bat in a bag by

a surgeon, a physician and a priest. While the surgeon made
an incision in the man's side – and the priest prayed – the
physician released the bat. The patient, convinced that the
force of evil had departed, recovered instantly.

# The swan's pure beauty

**Once the symbol of the Virgin Mary, the swan is a
bird of purity and beauty. Tales abound of swans being
transformed into lovely women, and vice versa.**

It is said in Ireland that the souls of virtuous maidens dwell
in swans. The birds pulled the chariots of Apollo and
Venus, and are said to be so sacred that to kill one is to bring
death upon the 'murderer' himself. In Greek legend, Zeus
transformed himself into a swan to seduce Leda, the mother
of Helen of Troy.

Of the many tales of swan maidens, typical is the one
in which a man, having seen a flock of swans alight on the
water and watched while they shed their feathers (revealing

**The swan** has long associations with kings. Edward I adopted it as a heraldic device and at the Feast of the Swan in 1306 his son took an oath on two swans with gilded beaks to avenge a murder committed by Robert the Bruce.

themselves as beautiful maidens), steals the robes of one of them. He marries her and all goes well until she discovers her feather dress in a cupboard, puts it on and disappears for ever.

The purity of the swan and the story of Leda were used by Edmund Spenser in his poem 'Prothalamion', which describes a pair of young brides as two swans:

*Two fairer Birds I yet did never see;*
*The snow which doth the top of Pindus strew*
*Did never whiter shew*
*Not Jove himselfe, when he a Swan would be,*
*For love of Leda, whiter did appeare;*
*Yet Leda was (they say) as white as he,*
*Yet not so white as these, nor nothing neare;*
*So purely white they were.*

# The victory eagle

**≫✦✦◄**

**The eagle, the 'king of birds', with super-keen eyesight, soaring flight and powerful beak and talons, usually with outspread wings, has always been held in the highest esteem and has been adopted as a symbol by rulers and nations down the ages.**

As the bird that represents triumph over evil, the eagle was sacred to Zeus. To show its power, which included immunity from lightning strikes, it was depicted holding both a snake and a thunderbolt and was revered as the equal of the sun. In the Hindu *Rig-Veda*, the eagle is the bringer to earth of the sacred soma, an intoxicating drink of divine power.

An eagle is said to have lifted, and then replaced, the helmet of Tarquinius Priscus, foretelling that he would become king of Rome – a prediction

**A SILVER EAGLE** was the icon of the Roman Republic, while a golden one symbolized the Roman Empire.

---

**EAGLE SYMBOLS**
- The Sioux sport eagle feathers in their war bonnets as a sign of victory.
- The American eagle was adopted as a national symbol in 1782.
- Poland's red eagle is depicted on a white background on the national flag.
- The Emperor Napoleon, who loved all things Roman, copied them by adopting the eagle as his symbol.
- The double-headed eagle was adopted as a national symbol by both Germany and Austria.

---

that came true in 616 BC. Roman legions, who used the eagle as their standard (because it was sacred to Jupiter), would set up winter quarters where there was an eagle's eyrie nearby.

# Bee messengers

**Whether flying singly or in swarms, bees are widely believed to be messengers of the gods and as such need to be kept happy and informed. As a swarm their behaviour may portend good or evil, depending on the circumstances.**

The most universal means of keeping bees happy (so that they will return to their hives and make honey) is to tell them at once of a death in the family. Recommended ways of doing this include tying black crape around the hive and bringing them food such as funeral biscuits soaked in wine or spicy funeral cake. They should also, it is said, be told of good news, as Rudyard Kipling advises in 'The Bee-boy's Song':

> *Marriage, birth or buryin'*
> *News across the seas,*
> *All your sad or merryin'*
> *You must tell the bees.*

Bees swarm as they follow a virgin queen out of the hive, at which time they can aggressively sting any human or animal who interferes with their determined journey to found a new colony.

Swarms of bees also make legendary appearances, as in the Irish story of the 6th-century St Gobnait: when her territory was being invaded she routed the enemy by holding up a small hive of bees, which swarmed and stung the invaders in the eyes, so blinding and dispersing them.

**GERMAN FOLKLORE** relates that bees were created so that they could supply wax for church candles. It was a common practice in medieval England for people to leave money in their wills to pay for the beeswax candles to light their funerals.

**Zeus, the father** of the Greek gods, was believed to have been born in a cave of bees and fed by them, and he was given the title Melissaios, or 'bee man'. Meliteus, Zeus's son, whose mother was a nymph, was hidden from Hera (Zeus's consort) in a wood and she was also nourished by bees.

# The helpful robin

**There are few more endearing birds than the robin redbreast, which is not afraid to come close to humans and their habitations. It is kindly regarded because of its legendary attention to the dying Jesus and its role as a bringer of fire.**

**ASSISTED BY THE WREN**, the robin was said to have covered the dead, unburied bodies of the Babes in the Wood with moss and leaves.

When, on Good Friday, a prickle from the crown of thorns was pressing deep into the Saviour's brow, the robin, it is said, flew to the Cross and tried to remove the thorn. As it was doing so, a drop of Christ's blood fell onto its breast, staining it forever. Another similar story ends with the bird injuring itself in its task, with the same result.

The robin is also renowned as the bird that brought fire to the world – but got its breast singed in the attempt. And according to Welsh legend the robin is red from being burned as it brought cooling waters to wicked souls being consumed by the fires of Hell. A verse by the early 19th-century poet John Greenleaf Whittier is based on this folktale:

**Because it is believed** to carry a drop of God's blood in its veins, it is extremely unlucky to kill a robin. Even an errant cat, it is said, will lose a limb if it murders this bird.

*'Nay,' said Grandmother, 'have you not heard
My poor bad boy, of the fiery pit,
And how drop by drop this merciful bird
Carries the water that quenches it?*

*'He brings cool dew in his little bill
And lets it fall on the souls of sin
You can see the marks on his
red breast still
Of fires that scorch as he drops it in.'*

# Hippo lore

**Often identified as the Behmoth of the Bible, the hippopotamus or 'water horse' is a symbol of power and strength. Recently, it has also become the subject of an urban legend.**

That the Egyptian word for the hippopotamus was *p-ehe-mau*, which became transmuted into the Hebrew word *b'hemah*, 'beast', is one of the theories behind the link between this creature and the huge animal that God described to Job. Behemoth represented the strength and intelligence that could deliver people from death:

> *What strength is in his loins!*
> *What power in the muscles of his belly!*
> *His tail is rigid as a cedar, the sinews of his flanks are tightly knit;*
> *His bones are like tubes of bronze, his limbs like iron bars.*

**A dwarf** named Od, so one of the top urban legends of 2005 relates, was swallowed by a circus hippopotamus in a freak accident in Thailand. One wayward bounce off a trampoline launched the dwarf into the animal's open jaws, which, by reflex, closed instantly.

The hippo's habit of living in the water during the day is explained in the Nigerian folktale of the hippo king called Isantim and his seven large, fat wives. Isantim held a feast for the other animals, but challenged them to tell him his name, and when they failed he sent them away. The tortoise asked what he would do if his name was discovered and the hippo said it would bring shame on him and he would leave the land to live in the river. While the hippo and his wives were bathing one day the tortoise overheard one of the wives calling his name. He revealed it at the next feast. The hippo, shamed by the discovery, went down to the water and stayed there, coming ashore only in darkness.

# The mighty elephant

**The elephant is so strong that even its image, carried as a talisman, is believed to confer similar power on the wearer. The creature's excellent memory, long renowned, is now a proven fact.**

In Indian tradition the earth is held in the universe by eight pairs of elephants which, when they grow tired and shake off their burden, cause earthquakes to occur. These creatures are named the Lokpalas. Hindus also believe that the warlike god Indra, symbol of prosperity and all-conquering temporal power, rode the earth on an elephant.

In African fables the elephant is the wise chief who impartially settles disputes among the forest creatures. One story is of a hunter who found an elephant skin near Lake Chad and hid it. Soon afterwards he spotted a large but beautiful girl crying because she had lost her 'clothes'. The hunter promised her new clothes and married her, and they had many large children. One day, when the family had run out of grain, the hunter's wife discovered her elephant skin hidden at the bottom of the barn. She put it on and went back to the bush to live as an elephant again. Her human sons became the ancestors of the clan who not only have the elephant as their totem but have nothing to fear from these creatures, who are their kin.

It is true that elephants have truly prodigious memories, especially for the odours of their enemies and members of their families. Each herd follows the routes or 'elephant roads' remembered in detail by the matriarch, the senior female.

 A 'WHITE ELEPHANT' is a euphemism for an unwanted object, especially one that is expensive to maintain. The expression comes from the rare, high-maintenance creatures given by the king of Siam (now Thailand) to those on whom he wished financial disaster.

# Dirty rats

### ❧

**The proverbial deserters of sinking ships, rats are generally reviled for their fecundity, destructive habits and their ability to carry disease.**

Shakespeare eloquently expresses the link between rats making their escape before a voyage and disaster at sea in *The Tempest,* when Prospero describes to Miranda how:

> *...they hurried us aboard a bark,*
> *Bore us some leagues to sea; where they prepar'd*
> *A rotten carcass of a boat, not rigg'd,*
> *Nor tackle, sail, nor mast; the very rats*
> *Instinctively had quit it.*

**The bad habits** of rats which 'fought the dogs and bit the cats,/And bit the babies in the cradles' were the subject of Robert Browning's poem 'The Pied Piper of Hamelin', in which the piper's playing lures both rats and children to their deaths.

Rats will gnaw anything, from computer cables to the traps set out to kill them, but they relish the garbage of human living. Most seriously, they are notorious as the vectors (with the help of fleas) of fatal diseases such as the Black Death of the Middle Ages (see Just a Flea Bite). Today, rats transmit Weil's disease, listeria, toxoplasmosis and possibly even SARS, a deadly variant of influenza.

A rat king is the name for a sinister phenomenon in which as many as 30 rats are bound together by their tails. Preserved specimens can be found in museums in Germany, Estonia and New Zealand. Such an occurrence is regarded as an evil omen, doubtless because of the association

**RATTY SAYINGS**

**The rat race** – the struggle to get ahead in business, whatever it takes.

**You dirty rat** – an expression famously attributed to the actor James Cagney. In fact in the 1932 movie *Taxi!* Cagney says to actor David Landau: 'Take that, you dirty yellow rat!'

**To rat on someone** – to tell tales about them, invariably to their detriment.

**King Rat** – the legendary 'leader of the pack'.

**'If you live in a city, you're probably in close proximity to two rats having sex right now'** – observation of American rat-watcher Robert Sullivan.

between rats and the plague. Rat kings have appeared in ovals including Terry Pratchett's *The Amazing Maurice and his Educated Rodents* in which the rats have a grudge against humanity. For the Venice Biennale in 1999 Katharina Fritsch created a rat king sculpture in plaster.

# A mouse in the house

### ❧❧

**Mice appear to be naturally timid because their keen eyesight and hearing, and sensitivity to vibrations, make them run for cover whenever danger threatens. Inhabitants of both town and country, they share our lives and homes.**

There are few more engaging descriptions of the habits of mice than Beatrix Potter's 'Appley Dapply':

*Appley Dapply, a little brown mouse,*
*Goes to the cupboard in somebody's house.*
*In somebody's cupboard there's everything nice,*
*Cake, cheese, jam, biscuits – all charming for mice!*
*Appley Dapply has little sharp eyes,*
*And Appley Dapply is so fond of pies!*

**TO BE AS QUIET** as a church mouse is to be silent for lack of food. Unlike a home, the church is devoid of tempting edibles.

Mice are said to embody the soul, which may leave the body during sleep in that form and even bring about a person's death. Even more ominously, mice are thought to be the inventions of witches, who make them out of pieces of cloth.

The silent daring of mice is celebrated by Aesop in his tale 'The Lion Who was Afraid of a Mouse, and the Fox' in which the fox rebukes the lion for fearing the mouse that 'ran all the way up his body' when he was asleep. In reply the lion says: 'It isn't that I was afraid of the mouse, but I was most surprised that there was anyone at all who could be so bold as to run along the body of a sleeping lion.' And the moral? Wise men don't ignore even little things. Unlike lions, domestic cats are the sworn enemies of mice, which is why, both proverbially and literally, when the cat's away, the mice will play.

# Bear strength

**Possessing superhuman strength and with a dangerous
propensity for unprovoked attack, the bear has long
been a symbol of power.**

The bear is sacred to many of the indigenous North
American people, and to the Ainu of Japan it was an
important ancestral figure. In Scandinavia the bear was deified
as Odin, chief of the gods and deity of wisdom and war. To
endow them with bear-like strength, Viking warriors, known
as Berserkers, wore bearskins into battle. The bearskins

worn today by Britain's Grenadier Guards were first captured from Napoleon's Imperial Guard at the Battle of Waterloo in 1815.

**SINCE THE 19TH CENTURY** the bear has frequently been used as a symbol of Russia, especially in the *Punch* cartoons of the 1870s drawn by Sir John Tenniel.

In the Old Testament, the two boys who shout after the prophet Elisha, 'Go up thou baldhead,' were punished with many others when 'there came forth two she-bears out of the wood and tore forty and two of them'. Before his encounter with Goliath, David killed bears and other wild animals with his sling, which symbolized his spiritual as well as his physical strength.

**For the Greeks** the bear was sacred to Artemis the huntress, and the creature was sacrificed to her. In one of her cults young women dressed as bears, probably for a pre-marriage initiation rite.

The teddy bear beloved of children is named for American President Theodore Roosevelt who famously refused to shoot a bear in a hunt and was subsequently lampooned for his action.

# The lion, king of the beasts

**Courage, strength and majesty are the attributes of the lion. Though it can be roused to anger, the lion also has a long-held reputation for magnanimity.**

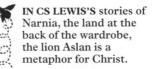

Statues of the king of beasts guarded the entrances to Egyptian tombs and palaces and sat astride the doors of Assyrian temples. As a symbol of the sun, the lion was linked with the Egyptian sun god Ra, the life giver. In today's London the lions sculpted by Sir Edwin Landseer 'guard' Trafalgar Square.

In Africa, where humans and lions have coexisted for millennia, the lion is revered as a reincarnation of dead ancestors, or a spirit that needs to be propitiated in some way.

**IN CS LEWIS'S** stories of Narnia, the land at the back of the wardrobe, the lion Aslan is a metaphor for Christ.

Some African people believe that men can be transformed into lions, thus becoming invulnerable to attacks by other animals. However to retain their status, they must leave part of any animals they kill as food for the lions.

The merciful character of the lion is well described by the Roman naturalist Pliny: 'Only the lion among wild animals shows mercy to suppliants; it spares those bent down before it, and, when angry, turns its rage on men rather than women, and only attacks children when desperately hungry.' In many stories, lions are renowned for their tenderness towards virgins. That the lion can forget its fierceness and lie down with the gentle lamb symbolizes the concept of peace in the Christian tradition. The same symbolism is used in Mughal art and in Naïve painting.

## Menacing big cats

**Although the lion and the tiger are both large cats, the tiger is never credited with the lion's saving graces. Nor is the leopard, which was once perceived as the animal embodiment of evil.**

Regarding the tiger with respect is only common sense, for of all the big cats it is the one most likely to be a maneater. In Sumatra, it is customary to offer formal apologies to such a creature before it is killed because, like other Asian peoples, Sumatrans believe that having eaten a man a tiger can subsequently make his ghost prowl the jungle and entice other victims to their deaths.

Other means of keeping the tiger

happy are never to speak of it disrespectfully and never to trespass on tiger trails. Keeping one's head covered also shows respect. At night, when the tiger's eyes are believed to shine, no sensible person would look back for fear of revealing apprehension to a potential attacker.

**Can a man** take on the tiger's might? Various traditional methods are tried, including eating tiger flesh – or, especially, its gall bladder – knotting a tiger whisker into your moustache or beard or carrying a tiger's claw in your pocket. You can also wear a 'tiger's eye', a semiprecious stone (a type of quartz), which glows golden brown. Roman soldiers are said to have worn them to distract their enemies.

# Monkey business

**It is their obvious similarity to humans that make monkeys and apes so intriguing and explain their association with mischief. Many of these creatures are thought to have special powers of wisdom.**

Playing on their resemblance to humans, a typical Creole folktale tells of Mr Monkey, who falls in love with a beautiful young girl. He dresses as a man and goes to call on her. One day he takes his best friend with him, who hints to the girl's father that there is a secret abroad, but will not reveal it. On Mr Monkey's wedding night the friend (who is jealous of Mr Monkey) sings a song that makes all monkeys dance, whether they wish to or not. Mr Monkey is forced to jump

**The Three Wise Monkeys**, covering their hands, ears and mouth, originated as an image carved above the portico of the Sacred Stable of the Nikko Toshogu Shrine, a 17th-century Japanese temple. Their motto, literally translated, reads: 'Don't see, don't hear and don't speak' and is popularly rendered as: 'See no evil, hear no evil and speak no evil.'

about so wildly that his tail comes out of his clothes, and his true identity is revealed. The father now understands what the secret is, and beats the bridegroom dreadfully, but the friend runs off, dancing and singing.

The Chinese Monkey King, Sun Wu-Kung is a master shape-shifter and his mischief-making even disrupts the peace of the gods, but he is instrumental in bringing Buddhism from India to China.

## MONKEY LANGUAGE

**Monkey business** – fooling about.

**Monkey puzzle** – a Chilean pine (*Araucaria araucana*), a tree with prickly branches that is said to be a puzzle even to an agile monkey.

**To monkey with** – to meddle with.

**Get one's monkey up** – to be irritable (as a monkey can be in life).

**Monkey nuts** – peanuts, perceived to be a food that monkeys enjoy.

# Fluttering by

**Both their fluttering flight and their life cycle have undoubtedly contributed to the notion that connects butterflies with the soul. Moths, however, have more sinister connotations.**

All over the world, the emergence of the butterfly from a dead-looking chrysalis is seen as a symbol of the soul leaving the body at the end of life. In some cultures the dead are believed to undergo a series of transformations before eventually coming back to life as butterflies.

Both butterflies and moths have connections with witches and bad things. Some say that the butterfly is the soul of a witch, but if it can be caught at night it will not be able to re-enter her evil body and will die. Moths are still often called witches and are believed to do evil deeds during the hours of darkness. Children were traditionally encouraged to kill them with hammers or at least catch them before they could steal the miller's grain.

Both angels and fairies are often depicted with butterfly wings, as is Psyche, the beautiful maiden loved by the immortal Eros, who visited her only in the dark so she should not know who he was. Fearing that he would not let her see him because he was a hideous monster, one night she lit a lamp while he was asleep to

**IT IS SAID** that to dream of a butterfly represents a wish to attain perfection or freedom from life's troubles.

**Shakespeare** used the butterfly to illustrate human fickleness when he wrote that 'men, like butterflies/Show not their mealy wings but to the summer.'

**IN AN EXPRESSION** of his agility and power in the ring, the boxer Muhammad Ali (formerly Cassius Clay) predicted that he would 'Float like a butterfly, sting like a bee.'

find out what her lover looked like. But a drop of hot oil fell on him and he woke and fled. Psyche then spent years a-flutter, searching for her love.

# The wisdom of salmon

**The salmon's long and arduous up-river journey to its spawning grounds is taken as evidence of its wisdom. This fish was once prized as the food of kings and only those of royal birth could eat it.**

**ST KENTIGERN,** patron saint of Glasgow, miraculously retrieved the lost ring of the Queen of Cadzow, finding it in the belly of a salmon.

The Irish legend of Fionn MacCumal tells how the warrior-to-be met the poet Finneces, who taught him the lessons of life. For seven years Finneces had been trying to catch the salmon of knowledge, which lived in a pool on the river Boyne: whoever ate the salmon would gain all the knowledge in the world. Eventually he caught it, and told the boy to cook it for him. While doing so Fionn burned his thumb, which he instinctively put in his mouth, and in so doing he swallowed a piece of the salmon's skin. He thus became imbued with the salmon's wisdom and from that day could call on it simply by sucking his thumb.

In western North America, where the salmon harvest was vital to the survival of the indigenous people, the leaping of salmon up massive rapids was explained by an earthquake, brought about by an evil spirit which, in trying to injure the people, blocked the fish's journey. The tribes of British Columbia constructed salmon 'ladders' for the fish to ascend, even resting on the rungs when exhausted. By setting salmon traps on these ledges, they could catch the fish easily.

**The uncanny,** almost supernatural, closeness of twins is explained in a North American legend that they were once salmon. For this reason twins are asked to use their voices to summon the fish and ensure a profitable harvest.

# The ways of the serpent

**Limbless, silent and deadly – it is easy to see how snakes have come to be symbols of evil. But they are also believed to be the embodiment of admirable attributes including wisdom and healing powers.**

As the Bible tells us, it was the serpent (which possessed the secrets of life) who, in the Garden of Eden, persuaded Eve to eat the forbidden fruit from the tree of knowledge, bringing sin into the world. God then cursed the creature, saying: 'You will crawl on your belly and you will eat dust all the days of your life.' In Christian art, the snake is often shown being crushed by the foot of Jesus, or at the foot of the cross, signifying Christ's triumph over sin. It is said that there are no snakes in Ireland because they were driven out by the good deeds of St Patrick.

**The concept** of the snake in the grass – embodying lurking, unseen evil – is an expression dating back to the poet Virgil.

The vanquishing of the evil serpent is a recurring theme. English legend relates how an abbess, St Hilda, rid the Yorkshire valley of Eskdale of its snakes by driving them to the edge of a cliff, then cutting off their heads with her whip. The ammonites (which are in fact fossilized shellfish) on the beach below are said to be the evidence of her success.

The link between the snake and healing may derive from the snake's ability to rejuvenate itself by sloughing off its skin. The snake was sacred to Asclepius, the Greek god of healing, whose shrines were guarded by sacred snakes. He was said to disguise himself as a serpent before carrying out his healing arts, and he is depicted, like his Roman counterpart Aesculapius,

**BECAUSE IT** can coil into a circle with its tail in its mouth, the snake represents eternity.

holding a staff with a snake entwined around it – which is still the physicians' symbol.

The wisdom of serpents meant that they were believed to have prophetic powers, and they were kept in Greek temples.

Many African tribal people share the belief that the souls of the dead reside in snakes, which is why the creatures visit houses. For this reason milk and food are often left out for them at night.

# Beetle power

**The behaviour of beetles – especially the scarab beetle – gave rise to their association with creation and renewal. They were sacred to the Egyptians, who believed that they had divine powers.**

The scarab or dung beetle (*Scarabeus sacer*) feeds on dung, which it rolls into a ball by pushing it along a slope with its hind legs. It then makes a hole in the ground, where it lodges the ball and begins to consume it. Both males and females do this, but the female may also remove a piece from the side of the ball where she lays her eggs, leaving a 'flap'. This led to the belief that new beetles were being created from the earth and, by inference, made the beetles divine, although the males were thought to be the actual 'creators'.

**Much to be feared** is the deathwatch beetle (*Xestibium rufovillosum*), whose larvae chew their way through structural timbers. The nocturnal adults betray their presence by a ticking sound that is heard in the quiet of a sleepless night – such as when keeping vigil beside a sickbed – and is believed to be an omen of impending death.

By extension, the scarab was thought to hide within itself the secret of eternal life and, as a result, images of scarabs were made and worn by the Egyptians for protection. Often heavily encrusted with jewels, these amulets were worn as pendants or rings. Most notable was the 'heart scarab', which was placed on the breast of a mummified dead body. Inscribed on it was a petition addressed by the dead person to his or her own heart, begging it not to bear witness against the deceased when it was weighed in judgement on the day of truth.

**THE EGYPTIAN SUN GOD** Ra was sometimes represented by a large black scarab sitting in the solar boat and rolling the sun's disk across the sky, another reference to the ball-forming habits of the scarab beetle.

# Cats, good and bad

**Over the centuries cats have been worshipped and revered, but also reviled as evil women in disguise. And they may bring good luck or bad, depending on colour and circumstance.**

Their natural instinct to catch and kill rats and mice endeared cats to the ancient Egyptians, for it was cats that kept precious granaries free from rodent ravages. On the death of a cat, Egyptian owners would even shave their eyebrows as a mark of respect. A lifeless creature's body would be taken to Bubastis, the city of the cat-headed goddess Bast or Pasht (who was believed to have nine lives) where it was embalmed in costly spices. To deliberately kill a cat was a crime that could warrant the death penalty. The Chinese, too, used cats to protect their silkworms from rats. Even images of 'silkworm cats' were thought to be effective if no live animals were to hand.

Cat colour is traditionally linked to fortune, though while black cats are lucky in Britain, elsewhere in Europe white ones are afforded this honour. A cat with fur in three colours (as in a tabby or tortoiseshell) was once thought to provide protection against fire.

**Reverence for the cat**, and the legend that a cat gave birth to kittens at the same moment as Christ was born, probably led to the animal's association with the Virgin Mary. Leonardo da Vinci was one of many artists who depicted a cat in scenes of the Virgin and Child.

The uncanny nature of cats certainly contributed to their link with witches – either as familiars or as these evil women in disguise. In some places it is still believed to be dangerous to discuss your most intimate secrets in a cat's presence. To test whether or not a cat really was a witch in disguise, it was an old custom to immerse the animal in holy water. If it attempted to escape then its evil nature was revealed.

**FREYA, the** Scandinavian goddess of love and fertility, travelled in a chariot drawn by cats.

The fixed, unblinking stare of the cat adds to its mystique. What's more, cats' eyes shine in the dark and their pupils contract and dilate hugely with changes in the intensity of light. Add to this their habits of hunting at night and you have an animal that is indubitably 'dark'.

---

### CAT CAUTIONS

Why cats need to be regarded with respect:
- If you kick a cat it will give you rheumatism.
- The Devil will haunt you if you kill a cat.
- A cat's purr is the sound of a ghost.
- It is extremely unlucky for a cat to die in your house.
- A cat's cough will be caught by everyone in the family.
- Cats can suck babies' breath and kill them.

# The faithful dog

***

**'Man's best friends', dogs are our companions and the guardians of our homes, appreciated for their faithfulness and trainability – the exact opposite of cats.**

The first dogs to be tamed were probably those drawn to the earliest human settlements where they could be guaranteed at least some scraps of leftovers. Soon they were not only guarding their human companions but being used in the hunting chase – like the 'greyhound' depicted pursuing a gazelle on a piece of Mesopotamian pottery some 8,000 years old.

'Beware the dog' (in Latin, *cave canum*), the inscription famously preserved from Pompeii after its destruction in 79AD, is testament to the Romans' appreciation of canine vigilance. As for companions, dogs were even bred by the Chinese at least 2,000 years ago to be tiny lap dogs, small enough to be slipped up a sleeve for winter warmth.

However dogs are also to be feared. Those that howl in the night are, by tradition, greatly feared as omens of death, and a dog seen scratching the earth was once deemed to be digging a grave – an event that would soon be followed by a death. In a vain attempt to effect a cure, people bitten by a rabid dog would eat the grass from a churchyard and apply dog's hair fried in oil and mixed with rosemary to the wound. Even a bite from a healthy dog might lead to the creature being put down as a precaution against madness.

For as long as they have been our companions, dogs have been helping to guard us and our property. Most fearsome of all guard dogs was Cerberus, the many-headed guard dog of Hades, who resided at the entrance to the underworld on the far side of the River Styx. There he prevented the souls or 'shades' of the dead from leaving; he also greeted the newly deceased as they arrived, sometimes amicably, but sometimes with ferocious snarling. To ensure that he remained in an amenable mood, the dead were provided with honey-cakes with which to placate the creature and keep him occupied as they passed.

---

**DOGGY SAYINGS**

The nature of the dog summed up by some of those know…

- 'The tiniest Poodle or Chihuahua is still a wolf at heart.' (Dorothy Hinshaw)
- 'To err is human, to forgive, canine.' (Anon)
- 'If you pick up a starving dog and make him prosperous, he will not bite you; that is the principal difference between a dog and a man.' (Mark Twain)
- 'The dog who barks furiously at a beggar will let a well-dressed man pass him without opposition.' (TH Huxley)

---

FOR
LOVE, LUCK
AND
HEALTH

*A*ll kinds of animals have been invoked over the ages to inspire romance, to avert ill fortune, and to bring good luck and better health. These animals' behaviour is even believed to be a way of predicting anything from the approach of bad weather to averting mishaps, disaster or even death. Simply carrying an animal's image about your person has long been believed to protect you from illness.

On the basis that some animals may be witches or evil spirits in disguise, they need to be met, greeted and treated with respect – or summarily destroyed. Rituals such as doffing a hat to a single magpie and telling news to bees have even evolved to counteract any malign influence that these creatures might have. On all kinds of occasions natural omens, such as birds flying into the house, are deemed important. So it is no surprise that the many superstitions relating to such events clearly reflect the close links between human lives and those of animals, particularly those we keep as pets or rear for their eggs or flesh. Even the constellations have, through animal depictions in horoscopes, become predictors of the future.

Although ancient medicine relied heavily on plant remedies, parts of animals – usually dead, but by no means always so – were also widely used. Often their application had more in common with sorcery than science, but the old fashioned uses of leeches and maggots have in fact regained a place in modern medical practice.

# Animal love signs

**Depending on how and when you meet them, and the way in which they behave, animals may be able to predict the course of true love.**

The spotted ladybird (or ladybug), which 'flies away home', is also believed to take wing to a true love. When you find the insect it should be gently blown off the hand or tossed into the air while chanting the words:

*Fly away east, fly away west,*
*Show me where lives the one I love best.*

Alternatively, you can use this old rhyme:

*Bishop, Bishop Barnabee,*
*Tell me when my wedding be;*
*If it be tomorrow day,*
*Take your wings and fly away.*

**A bizarre old custom** is throwing a herring membrane. Along the underside of the fish is a small strip of fat. A girl would remove this and throw it at a wall. If it landed upright, then her husband would be equally admirable, but a membrane that landed in a crooked fashion denoted a dishonest partner.

On St Valentine's Day, young women would peer through the keyhole of the house. If they saw a cock and a hen they could be sure to be wed within the year. In spring, they would count the calls of the first cuckoo, the number of calls being the years until marriage.

Even snails can be called on for the purposes of divination. When every home had an open fire, Shropshire girls were advised: 'Take a black snail by the horns, and throw it over your shoulder on to the hearth at night. In the morning, its slimy trail among the ashes will show the initials of your future husband.'

# Money and wealth

**Nearly all of us wish, if not for wealth, at least for enough money to be 'comfortable'. If you read the signs of the natural world correctly, riches may indeed come your way.**

When you hear the first cuckoo call of the season turn the money in your pocket and spit on it. And remember the old saying, 'Who eats oysters on St James's Day will never want.' (The saint's day, 25 July, once marked the beginning of the oyster season.)

Animals you encounter can also confer wealth. A frog is a sign of money (in Scotland a prudent housewife might even keep one in the cream bowl). And if, on the way to conduct important business, a black and white spotted dog crosses your path, you will meet with success. If you see the first lamb of spring facing you, it signifies a diet of meat for the rest of the year – and the money to afford it. But if you see

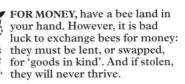

**FOR MONEY,** have a bee land in your hand. However, it is bad luck to exchange bees for money: they must be lent, or swapped, for 'goods in kind'. And if stolen, they will never thrive.

the creature's tail first you will eat only milk and vegetables. Similarly, if the first butterfly you see in spring is white then you will eat white bread for the rest of the year. Conversely, a brown butterfly means brown bread, traditionally associated with poverty.

# The lucky greeting

**Meeting – and greeting – animals and birds may bring good luck, depending on how you do it. Old superstitions often demand the reciting of verse, or even elaborate actions to ward off evil.**

The evil powers of bats, widely viewed as agents of death and the Devil, or witches in disguise, certainly need to be assuaged. One old way is to chant a protective verse such as this one:

*Airy mouse, airy mouse fly over my head,*
*And you shall have a crust of bread;*
*And when I brew and when I bake,*
*You shall have a piece of my wedding cake.*

The magpie, said to be coloured black and white because it refused to go into full mourning after the Crucifixion, may be unlucky or the reverse, according to the old rhyme (which has several versions):

*One for sorrow, two for mirth,*
*Three for a wedding, four for a birth,*
*Five for silver, six for gold,*
*Seven for a secret, not to be told,*
*Eight for heaven, nine for Hell*
*And ten for the Devil's own sell [self].*

There are many traditional ways of dispelling the ill luck of seeing one magpie. You may, bow and say aloud 'Good morning to you Mr Magpie, Sir,' or 'Good magpie, magpie, chatter and flee, turn up thy tail and good luck fall me.' You may remove your hat, or spit over your right shoulder and say 'Devil, Devil I defy thee,' or make the sign of the cross on the ground. An onion kept in the pocket gives all-day protection from single magpies. And should you see a single bird flying away from the sun, defy bad luck by throwing something after it.

**DISPEL the bad luck** of a crow by saying, 'Crow, crow, get out of my sight/Or else I'll eat thy liver and lights.'

# Harm them at your peril

Certain birds – and some insects – are so 'charmed'
or sacred that causing harm to them in any way can
bring disaster. Some of these creatures are also greatly
feared for their malign potential.

Deliberately killing a robin portends a life of doom. For a
farmer it means that his cows will give bloody milk and
his barns will catch fire. This is because the robin is revered
as a bird with Christian connections and is believed to be
protective and helpful, as in this ballad recounting the death
of the Babes in the Wood:

> *No burial this pretty pair*
> *From any man receives.*
> *Till robin redbreast piously*
> *Did cover them with leaves.*

Swans, birds associated in myth with the white clouds that formed the chariot of the Norse sun god Freyr, are deemed sacred throughout northern Europe. In Britain all swans are protected by law. Swallows, which return year after year to the same nesting places in homes and barns, can consider themselves safe because it's believed that destroying their nests would bring harm to the buildings from fire or lightning. It is said that even cats know that it is unlucky to kill a swallow.

**Insects** that should be afforded respect include ladybirds (ladybugs or ladybeetles). Dubbed by some 'God almighty's Cows', they should be released (or buried if accidentally killed) while chanting the rhyme: 'Ladybird, ladybird fly away home,/ Your house is on fire and your children are gone.' It is also unlucky to kill an ant because it is said to embody the soul of an unbaptized child – or a fairy transformed into a human.

**NEVER KILL** a coyote or you may lose your wits. Killing a cat may shorten your life.

# Prediciting stormy weather

**The behaviour of birds and animals has long been thought to predict the weather. When it comes to storms, the petrel and the cat take centre stage.**

Except when they are breeding, many storm petrels (*Oceanites oceanicus*) live entirely at sea, feeding on plankton, krill and fish. To superstitious sailors, their

**Hovering close** to the ocean surface, storm petrels look as though they are 'walking' on the waves, which may explain why they are often called St Peter's birds, because Peter followed Jesus's command to walk on water. Another theory is that the name comes from their 'pitter-pattering' on the water. They are also called 'Mother Carey's chickens', supposedly from the words '*Mata cara*', or 'Dear mother', uttered by sailors when storms strike.

appearance bodes ill, often rightly so, because they follow ships in stormy weather, scavenging for food scraps.

Both cats and petrels are widely believed to take on the guise of witches and to cause – and ride on – storms. To protect sailors, cats ashore would be shut up in cupboards. Even uttering the word 'cat' is still taboo among Scottish sailor folk.

## CATS AT SEA

Some superstitions linking cats and storms:

- Cats can start storms through magic stored in their tails, which is why sailors always make sure that they are well fed and contented.
- If a cat licks its fur against the grain a hailstorm is coming; if it sneezes, rain is on the way; and if it is frisky, the wind will soon get up.
- Throwing a cat overboard is a sure way of raising a storm.
- Fishermen's wives keep black cats at home to prevent storms and other disasters at sea.

# Animals at home

**From snakes to sparrows, creatures that come into the home can presage good or ill, depending on their identity and the way they behave.**

In countries where they are indigenous, snakes that come into the house are generally thought to be lucky. As well as generally bringing good fortune, they are believed to embody the souls of ancestors, and to be guardian spirits that watch over the members of the family, especially children. In Armenia a snake that arrives in the night is offered food and drink – the hospitality any stranger would be afforded. Similarly, the sudden departure of a house snake is said to presage misfortune. The sloughed skin of a snake, hung up in the house, is thought to make it fireproof.

**WELCOME ROOKS** who nest in trees near your home – they are said to bring good luck; but beware if they desert their rookery, for then bad luck may befall.

Like house snakes, sparrows may also contain the souls of the departed. If they fly into the house they are said to presage death. That sparrows should be treated with caution is summed up in the old rhyme: 'The spink [chaffinch] and the sparrow/Are the Devil's bow and arrow.'

# Birds of doom

❧

**Once revered as messengers of the gods, and endowed with powers of flight denied to mere mortals, birds and their behaviour have strong links with the foretelling of death. The ways in which birds behave around a home are, to the superstitious, significant death predictors.**

Most to be feared are a bird that flies into the house through an open window or down the chimney, a bird tapping on the window or one hovering over the house. You also need to listen for the calls that birds make, especially at unusual times. Cocks crowing late at night, ravens croaking between 10 o'clock and midnight and a cuckoo that calls after August are all believed to presage death.

**TWO LARGE WHITE BIRDS**, the size and shape of albatrosses, are said to fly over Salisbury Cathedral when the death of the incumbent bishop is imminent.

Certain places and families have had particular reasons to fear the appearance of birds. The Oxenham family of Devon long believed that when someone fell ill they would be sure to die if a white-breasted bird appeared in the bedroom and hovered over the sick bed before disappearing.

The numbers and positions in which birds are seen can also be significant. Single magpies, ('One for sorrow'), while generally unlucky, are not as bad as a whole flock seen flying past the house. A single white pigeon on a roof is a death omen, as are three seagulls seen flying close together.

**MORE AVIAN OMENS**
Expect a death in the family if:
- A swallow alights on you.
- A pigeon settles on your kitchen table.
- You meet a vulture.
- Hens lay eggs with double yolks.
- A cock crows all day and night.

# Christmas lore

**Animals may augur good luck or bad at Christmas time. They play an important part in many ancient customs, and it is a widespread belief that the descendants of those who were present at the Nativity still show their deference on Christmas night.**

*Christmas Eve, and twelve of the clock.
'Now they are all on their knees,'
An elder said as we sat in a flock
By the embers in hearthside ease.*

*We picture the meek mild creatures where
They dwelt in their strawy pen,
Nor did it occur to one of us there
To doubt they were kneeling then.*

So Thomas Hardy viewed the kneeling of the cattle in midnight homage; their breath is averred to be sweet because it warmed the

**Bees hum** a sacred hymn on Christmas Eve. After the calendar changed by 11 days in 1752 (not to everyone's pleasure) people would listen on both the 'old' and 'new' Christmas to make sure that they could hear it – and to reveal the 'true' date of Christmas.

infant Jesus. Sheep, also, are said to turn to the east and bow at this hour, and it is deemed especially lucky to meet a flock at this time of year. The power of the crowing cock to dispel evil spirits which, like the ghost of Hamlet, fade 'on the crowing of he cock', is particularly potent at Christmas, when it is said to raise its voice all night long.

Old Christmas country rituals involved parading animal effigies in the streets. In Dorset (where it was called the Ooser) and Wiltshire, a terrifying bull's head mask was worn by a man swathed in sacking, who demanded refreshment from anyone he met. In Kent a horse's head on a pole was paraded, demanding drinks and money: 'If ye the hooden horse doth feed,/Throughout the year thou shalt not need.'

 **EVEN TO TALK** of a wolf during the 12 days of Christmas may bring bad luck.

# Easter rites

**The original 'Easter bunny' was in fact a hare. The link goes back to pre-Christian times, when this creature was sacred to the Anglo Saxon goddess Eastre, after whom the festival was named.**

Once revered as holy, the hare was associated with fertility and the return of spring, and by tradition it is the hare that lays the brightly coloured eggs hidden for children to hunt on Easter morning. The benevolence of the hare at this season was at odds, however, with the widely held idea that hares were witches in disguise. It was extremely unlucky to meet one and to do so was even thought to put your life into severe danger.

At their spring festivals the ancient Greeks and Romans exchanged coloured eggs and today hard boiled, painted eggs (dyed red in some countries to signify the spilt blood of Christ) still represent Easter's promise. One Polish legend relates that that eggs were first painted by Mary to amuse the infant Jesus. Easter eggs are put into the fields to encourage god crops and protect them from hail and thunder, and in some places one may be kept in the house as a protective amulet.

# Beware the owl

❧

**Although revered for its wisdom, the owl – with its nightly hooting and predatory habits – is also feared.**

**In Ethiopia** it was an old custom that when a guilty man was condemned to death he was carried to a table on which an owl was painted. On seeing the bird he was expected to kill himself.

Owls are thought by many to be witches in disguise (and witches used parts of the birds' bodies in their 'brews'). They are especially loathed when seen flying in the daytime, and when they raise their voices. Hearing a screech owl hooting three times is thought to be a death omen. As in the cases of bats and magpies, the power of the sound can be dispelled with an appropriate action, as in this verse from the southern United States:

*When you hear the screech owl, honey, in the sweet gum tree,*
*It's a sign as sure as you're born a death is bound to be;*
*Unless you put the shovel in the fire mighty quick,*
*For to conjure that old screech owl, take care the one that's sick.*

When an owl is seen flying around the house, perching on the roof or, worst of all flying down the chimney, the omens are bad and a family death is likely, though killing the bird may dispel bad luck. Shakespeare's Lady Macbeth hears the ominous hoot of an owl while she perpetrates her bloody deed.

---

**MORE OWL LORE**
• If you look into an owl's nest you will be unhappy for the rest of your life.
• An owl hoots every time a girl loses her virginity.
• A pregnant woman who hears an owl hoot will give birth to a girl.
• If you hear an owl hoot when a baby is born the child will be ill-fated.

---

# Forecasting the weather

**The calls and behaviour of birds and animals were once among the country dweller's most important weather forecasters, and were taken seriously at such vital times as haymaking and harvest.**

There is at least a modicum of fact to support some bird omens. In Scotland, for instance, where the frequent calling of a cuckoo is a sign of rain, it is true that episodes of poor weather – known as 'gowk storms' – coincide with the birds' arrival in spring. It is also thought that birds are sensitive to the atmospheric changes that precede rain, hence the

**The chirping** of crickets is a sign of impending rain – and more. The 19th-century naturalist Gilbert White observed: 'They are the housewife's barometer, foretelling her when it will rain; and are prognostic sometimes, she thinks, of ill or good luck; of the death of a near relation, or the approach of an absent lover.'

rhymes, 'When the peacock loudly bawls/Soon we'll have both rain and squalls,' and 'If the cock goes crowing to bed/He'll certainly rise with a watery head.'

Though it may not actually rain, seeing swallows flying low means that the air is damp and their insect prey are flitting near the ground. Larks fly high in the air when the weather is destined to stay fine.

---

**BELIEVE IT IF YOU WILL**

According to ancient lore, expect rain (maybe) if:
- Asses bray.
- Fleas bite more than usual.
- Rooks sit in rows on walls or fences.
- A black snail crosses your path.
- Swans take to the air.
- Spiders anchor their webs with short threads.
- Pigs rush around with straws in their mouths.
- A cat washes over its ears.

# Groundhog Day and Candlemas

Predicting the arrival of spring is associated with Candlemas on 2 February, 40 days after Christmas, which is the feast of the Purification of the Virgin. In America it is Groundhog Day, when one animal's behaviour is closely observed.

The roots of Candlemas go back to at least the 6th century, when it was taken to be the middle of winter, after which the sun's intensity begins to increase significantly. The bear and badger may make brief forays out of hibernation at this time, but the groundhog has been inextricably linked with Candlemas since 1886, when Clymer Freas, the editor of the *Punxsutawney Spirit* of western Pennsylvania, reported that, because the groundhog had emerged – but not seen his shadow – that day, there would be an early spring. Conversely, the emerging animal witnessing its shadow in the sunshine predicts another six weeks of winter.

**CANDLEMAS is** so named because it is the day when the church candles to be used for the rest of the year are blessed.

The prognosticating groundhog is often known as Punxutawney Phil, and his predictions follow a European Candlemas tradition brought to Pennsylvania by German settlers in the 18th century.

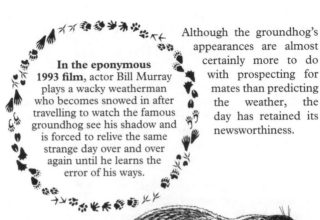

**In the eponymous 1993 film,** actor Bill Murray plays a wacky weatherman who becomes snowed in after travelling to watch the famous groundhog see his shadow and is forced to relive the same strange day over and over again until he learns the error of his ways.

Although the groundhog's appearances are almost certainly more to do with prospecting for mates than predicting the weather, the day has retained its newsworthiness.

# Creatures of the zodiac

**The creatures that feature in the zodiac relate to the constellations that bear their names. The characteristics of people born under these animal signs are believed to reflect those animals' temperaments.**

Astrology, one of the oldest forms of divination, began when people first tried to make links between the positions of the stars in the sky and the cycle of the seasons. Today astrology makes its predictions on the basis of the positions of certain constellations at the moment and place of a person's birth, and their conjunction with the sun, moon and planets.

The practice of astrology as we now know it was begun by the Babylonians who imagined the zodiac or 'belt' in which the constellations were contained. The stars, sun and moon travelled, they believed, in three celestial 'wheels', at whose centre was the pole star.

**In medieval cosmology**, everything was composed of the four elements, earth, air, fire and water, and each zodiacal sign was allotted to one of these. No animal signs represent air, the realm of intellect and imagination, but Aries and Leo exhibit the intensity of fire, Taurus and Capricorn share the stability of earth, and the water signs, Cancer, Scorpio and Pisces, show emotion and intuition.

**THE DATES** assigned to each sign are those when the sun is said to enter it, representing an imaginary situation in which, were the sun viewed at the same time as the constellation, its stars would be surrounding the solar orb.

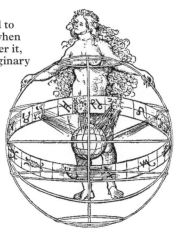

# Aries – the ram

The courage and spirit of the ram are reflected in the characteristics of Arians, born between 21 March (the spring equinox) and 18 April. They are said to be idealists with implicit faith in their abilities and any causes they choose to espouse, but they also have fiery tempers.

Their love of domination is said to make Arians hard partners to live with and strict disciplinarians, but they excel wherever they can organize, take the lead and give rein to their intellectual powers. Their natural bent is to be guided by their instincts, though they are not noted for scheming or subtlety. Unable to be led or compelled, Arians may be easily deceived by praise or flattery – and will express their anger forcefully if found out.

That Aries is the first sign of the zodiac relates to the Mesopotamian myth that the world was created at the moment the sun entered this constellation. The Ram in the sky was believed to hold within it the stars of the winter solstice. It was no coincidence that in ancient Babylon the month following the spring equinox was the season in which rams, the prime symbols of the male generative force in a pastoral society, were offered as sacrifices to the gods.

# Taurus – the bull

The bull is an animal symbolic of fertility and power, associated with both the arrival of spring rains and with Zeus, king of the gods. The birth dates for Taurus are 19 April to 20 May.

It was Taurus the heavenly bull who, according to the ancient Sumerians and Babylonians, brought the vernal equinox. This was the bull created by the sky god Anu (a creature whose bellowing was said to cause thunderclaps) to confront the epic warrior hero Gilgamesh. To the Greeks, Taurus was Zeus in disguise. Appearing from the sea, he lured Europa to climb on his back and abducted her to Crete, where a bull cult became prevalent.

Taureans are lovers of beauty and nature, but no matter how vivid their flights of fancy may be, they temper these with common sense. Though slow to anger, they will, when roused, display massive wrath, and they are equally tardy in forgetting sleights. They shun deception and underhand dealings, naturally adopt leadership roles and revel in work that links them with the earth and with animals.

**SOME EARLY** Christian astronomers associated Taurus with the ox which, in the Bethlehem stable, witnessed the birth of Christ.

# Cancer - the crab

From 21 June to 22 July the sun is in the sign of Cancer, considered a 'sensitive' sign. The sign was named after the crab because, at the summer solstice (technically now in Gemini), the sun appeared to move sideways across the sky.

Astronomically, the most significant part of the constellation is a cluster of stars named the Beehive. The Chaldeans called this the Gate of Men and believed it to be the entrance taken by souls leaving heaven to take up residence in human bodies. To the Greeks, the crab was the creature that bit the feet of Hercules as he wrestled the Hydra. Though killed by the hero, the creature was rewarded by Hercules' enemy Hera (the wife of Zeus) with a place in the heavens. That the constellation appears faint, with no one bright star, is a reminder of its inauspicious end.

Like the crab, Cancereans are timid and hesitant, but tenacious. Those born under this sign are enormously sensitive, especially to criticism, and anxious over the small things in life. However they are shrewd with money (though poor gamblers) and have excellent memories. Family matters greatly to them. As befits association with a marine creature they are good sailors and happy at sea.

**The Roman naturalist** Pliny said that when the sun was in the sign of Cancer dead crabs lying on the sand would turn into serpents. Storms, famine and locusts were also once linked with this conjunction.

# Leo – the lion

From 23 July to 22 August the sun is in the constellation of Leo, the fifth sign of the zodiac. As positive and noble as the lion, Leos are forceful and direct, though also extremely affectionate.

One of the first astrological signs to be recognized, Leo was identified with the lion by all the major ancient civilizations and coincided, originally, with the heat of the summer solstice. In Egypt, the sun in Leo was a time when the Nile flooded, so ensuring the coming year's fertility, but it was also when lions actually appeared.

The lion has many resonances in mythology. Leo may have been the Sumerian monster Humbaba, who guarded the forest of cedars where the gods resided. It was also linked with Nergal, a god of war and pestilence commonly portrayed with a lion's body.

THE NEMEAN LION killed by Hercules was the Leo of the Greek world. It is thought to have been translated into the Judeo-Christian tradition as the lion defeated by the Old Testament hero Daniel.

Simple nobility, combined with courage, are the characteristics of Leos, who are said to be strangers to fear. Their directness can make them tactless, and they can be severe in manner, even to those they love and admire. They are particularly quick to take offence if they think that their honour and dignity is being challenged in any way. Many Leos become leaders and statesmen and as such may command great devotion.

# Scorpio – the sting in the tail

**Extremes and contradictions are the outstanding attributes of Scorpios, born between 23 October and 21 November. Like the creatures whose constellation they share these humans have an infamous sting in the tail.**

**The Maoris** of New Zealand call the constellation of Scorpio the Fish-hook of Maui, and it is believed to have caught their islands and heaved them up from the depths of the ocean.

Orion, the giant hunter of Greek mythology renowned for his good looks, was stung to death by Scorpio. This monster also terrified the horses of the sun when they were being driven across the heavens by Phaethon, with the result that he lost control of his chariot, which then careered across the sky scorching the Milky Way in its path. This sign is traditionally associated with cold and darkness, and even with the start of wars and other evil deeds. In ancient times the only people who relished the sun in this sign were alchemists, who believed that is was the only time when they could convert base metals into gold.

Talented but inclined to vanity, tenacious but biting and given to tempers, Scorpios will champion the weak and oppressed, and show little regard for convention. They are ambitious – often ruthless – and remarkable achievers. The are gifted actors, whether in the theatre or merely on life's stage, but often give totally the wrong impression of their character and temperament. They are intensely loving, but can also be extraordinarily secretive and jealous.

# Capricorn – the goat

**Between 22 December and 19 January, immediately following the winter solstice, the sun is in Capricorn, the sign of the goat, an animal noted for its persistence in ascending to the mountain tops.**

In assessing its place in the heavens, the Chaldean astronomers of ancient Assyria assigned Capricorn to the 'Sea', a group of constellations that they believed represented the army of monstrous creatures who protected Tiamat, a huge female dragon and the primordial mother. The goat was endowed with the tail of a fish, a characteristic the Greeks later explained as a result of the goat-footed god Pan being frightened by the appearance of the 'wind monster' Typhon and leaping into the water.

**PLACED DIRECTLY OPPOSITE** Cancer in the zodiac, Capricorn was the other Gate of the Gods, and the one through which souls passed on their journey from earth to heaven.

Capricorns are noted for being hard-working, shrewd and calculating, also reserved and often secretive. They are painstaking and methodical – stopping at nothing to achieve the goals that they have set themselves – and, having supreme faith in their own abilities, are natural leaders and good communicators. By reputation they are tactful and slow to anger but equally tardy in forgetting any wrongs done to them, which can make them jealous and even vengeful.

# Pisces – a fishy duo

**The symbol of Pisces is a pair of fishes, which, although attached to each other, are moving in opposite directions, typifying those born between 19 February and 20 March.**

**Pisces** is the sign said to control the weather and, by inference, the fate of sailors. Although generally a bringer of bad luck, its links with rain made it, to early civilizations, a fertile sign.

In the heavens, the two constellations of Pisces are connected with strings of stars that look like ribbons. The Romans believed that when the love goddess Venus and the vain Cupid (who inspired her jealousy by falling in love with Psyche) were chased by Typhon they ended up in the sky. In Christian symbolism the fish are the two which (with the five loaves) Jesus fed the multitude.

Pisceans are renowned for their dual nature. While intending to do one thing they in fact do another. With wide vision and rich imaginations they may dream up the wildest, most grandiose schemes but, when faced with reality, find themselves unable to put these into action. Romantic, kind hearted and emotional, Pisceans are sensitive to rebuffs, though with the right guidance and backing they can achieve great things. They are also good learners and readily accumulate knowledge.

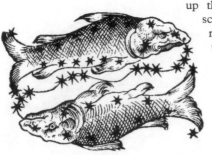

# Chinese astrology

**Like its western equivalent, the Chinese system of astrology classifies people according to 12 signs. However, all are animal forms and the sign to which you are ascribed depends on the year (according to the Chinese calendar) in which you were born.**

This ancient perspective on our modern lives comes from the ancient Oriental art of divination and character reading. Legend has it that the Buddha invited all the animals to a New Year party, but from the whole world only 12 made the effort to come. He was so touched by their attendance that he gave each the gift of a year, beginning with the party-loving rat and ending with the pig.

The day on which each year of the cycle begins is determined by the moon, so the exact date changes every year. Overlaying the 12-year cycle of animal signs there is also a 60-year cycle, linking each animal with one of five basic elements: fire, earth, metal, water and wood.

# CHINESE ZODIAC ANIMAL CHARACTERS

**Rat** – ambitious, hardworking leaders, often charming to the opposite sex. Enjoy gossiping. Best with Ox, Monkey and Dragon (Years: 1936, 1948, 1960, 1972, 1984, 1996, 2008, 2012…)

**Ox** – responsible and hard-working, but can be bigoted, stubborn and absolutely assured they are right. Best with Rat, Snake and Rooster. (Years: 1937, 1949, 1961, 1973, 1985, 1997, 2009, 2021…)

**Tiger** – charismatic and courageous, deep thinkers but can be indecisive and sensitive. May be apt to show off. Best with Dog, Horse and Dragon. (Years: 1938, 1950, 1962, 1974, 1986, 1998, 2010…)

**Rabbit (Hare)** – financially lucky, funny, articulate, artistic and diplomatic. Peace-loving, slow to lose their tempers. Best with Dog, Goat and Bear. (Years: 1939, 1951, 1963, 1975, 1987, 1999, 2011…)

**Dragon** – vibrant, optimistic and brave. Inspire trust and confidence in others, but also judgemental and egotistical. Best with Rat, Snake, Rooster and Monkey. (Years: 1940, 1952, 1964, 1976, 1988, 2000, 2012…)

**Snake** – wise and confident, passionate but reserved, mysterious and evasive. Hate to fail. Thrifty and financially lucky. Best with Ox, Rooster and Dragon. (Years: 1941, 1953, 1965, 1977, 1989, 2001, 2013…)

**Horse** – talented, wise, cheerful and adventurous, with many friends but slow to take advice. Best with Dog, Tiger and Goat. (Years: 1942, 1954, 1966, 1978, 1990, 2002, 2014…)

**Goat (Ram or Sheep)** – artistic and graceful, animated, romantic and popular, but beneath the surface may be shy, insecure and awkward. Best with Horse, Boar and Rabbit. (Years: 1943, 1955, 1967, 1979, 1991, 2003, 2015…)

**Monkey** – brilliant and curious, good problem solvers. Have excellent memories but can be impatient for results. Best with Rat and Dragon. (Years: 1944, 1956, 1968, 1980, 1992, 2004, 2016…)

**Rooster** – efficient and ambitious. Deep thinkers, but also enthusiastic, stubborn and vain with a good sense of humour. Best with Snake, Dragon and Ox. (Years: 1945, 1957, 1969, 1981, 199, 2005, 2017…)

**Dog** – intensely loyal and honest, also witty and animated. A great friend, but also pessimistic and afraid of rejection, often finding fault. Best with Tiger, Rabbit and Horse. (Years: 1946, 1958, 1970, 1982, 1994, 2006, 2018…)

**Pig (Boar)** – generous and affectionate. Quiet, but with a thirst for knowledge and able to face life's problems head-on. Best with Goat and Rabbit. (Years: 1947, 1959, 1971, 1983, 1995, 2007, 2019…)

# Dreams and prophecies

**Of all forms of divination, the interpretation of dreams is among the oldest. In the Bible, the Pharaoh's dream, interpreted by Joseph, was crucial to the fate of the Israelites in Egypt.**

**In dreams** that feature animals, their significance often relates directly to the character of the creature. Dreams of domestic animals are thought, in general, to mean happiness, while those of wild predators such as lions and tigers signify cruel and treacherous enemies.

As Genesis relates, Pharaoh saw in his first dream 'seven cows, sleek and fat' followed by 'seven other cows, gaunt and lean', which devoured the seven fat animals. In his second dream he saw 'seven ears of grain, full and ripe', then after them 'seven other ears, thin and shrivelled', which swallowed up the plump ears.

Since his own counsellors could not help him, Pharaoh sent for Joseph, who told him that the seven good cows and ears of grain represented fertile years; the thin cattle and weedy grains meant seven years of famine. He advised frugality and saving during the good years, to counter the effects of the bad. So impressed was the Pharaoh that he gave him 'authority over the whole land of Egypt'.

# Healing the stomach

**In the days long before refrigeration, when digestive illnesses were rife, especially in warm countries, wearing an amulet to ward them off was common practice. Many of the motifs evoked the healing power of animals and birds.**

The ibis, often shown on an altar, and possibly tethered to papyrus reeds, was favoured as a talisman for healing ailments of the stomach. This bright red bird with its long, curved beak, sacred to the Egyptian god Thoth, was reputed to be able to devour serpents, reptiles and other harmful vermin. Greek amulets for the stomach were often heart-shaped or oval pieces of jasper, the grey-green mineral steatite or dark brown limonite, bearing inscriptions such

as 'Good digestion' or simply 'Digest!'

The iconic image of a *chnoubis* – a thick-bodied snake with a lion's head encircled by projecting rays

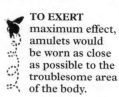

**TO EXERT** maximum effect, amulets would be worn as close as possible to the troublesome area of the body.

– was also thought to improve digestive health, especially when it was carved into a piece of green jasper. This was thought to be effective by no lesser authority than Galen, the Greek physician, who claimed to have tested it personally.

# To cure a fever

**Fevers or agues, often the heralds of fatal diseases such as typhoid, smallpox and scarlet fever, were once rightly dreaded. No wonder, then, that 'animal magic' was widely used to cure them.**

**Eating a live spider** embedded in an apple, or in a spoonful of jam or treacle, is an old fever remedy. Hanging a 'necklace' of spiders around a fever patient until the animals died was a more drastic variation. Another was shutting a spider in a box until it expired.

That a fever (or other illness) could be transferred to a passing animal was once a common superstition. Cats – and dogs – were widely used for this purpose. Typically, an entry in *Notes & Queries* of 1892 relates: 'All my family being laid up with the influenza [we]…proposed to cut off some hair from the hollow of the neck, put it in milk, and give it to an animal to drink… The disease would then be transferred to the animal, and the patient would recover...'

More drastic yet was a midwife's advice of 1888: 'If the baby is ill and not thriving, take a cat by the four feet, swing it round and round the infant several times then throw it out of the hole in the roof for letting out the smoke; if it is a black cat...then throw the cat out of the window; if the cat dies the child will live...'

Passing a fevered child under an ass's belly three times was another way of bringing about a cure. This was most effective if the animal first ate some bread or a biscuit out of the child's lap.

**BIZARRE FEVER REMEDIES** include skinning a male mole, drying and powdering the pelt, then drinking it mixed with gin – or rubbing the soles of the feet with half a pigeon.

# The dreaded cough

Whooping cough, now largely avoided by immunization, was once a fatal disease that families feared. The characteristic sound of the cough was often significant to the suggested cure.

As with fevers, the healing power of asses was commonly used to treat whooping cough, not least because of the similarity in sound of the animal's braying and the noise made by the patient. Nine hairs taken from the white cross marking on a she-animal's back were hung in a bag around the child's neck.

In some places children would be placed on asses' backs as soon as they were old enough, with the idea that this would protect them from catching the disease. And because of the luck firmly associated with his mount, anyone riding a piebald horse was automatically consulted by anyone seeking a cure for the whooping cough.

## MORE CURES

According to old superstitions, you could cure whooping cough by:

- Hanging a frog (because its croaking sounded like the cough) in the chimney.
- Putting a black beetle, a frog or a spider in a box and hanging it round the patient's neck. As the creature died, then decayed, so the illness would disappear.
- Drinking milk in which a live trout had been made to swim.

# Blood letting leeches

The idea of curing patients by letting leeches suck their blood began in Egypt some 2,500 years ago. The practice has now been revived to help prevent blood clotting in patients immediately following surgery.

Bloodletting by leeches (zoologically related to earthworms), thought to be able to cure everything from obesity and laryngitis to mental illness, reached its height in the 1800s. The Victorian self-help manual *Enquire Within* equipped its readers with the practical knowledge to use leeches for themselves. It

**Bloodletting by leeches** was thought to restore the balance of the four humours – blood, phlegm, black bile and yellow bile – on which Western medicine was based from the time of the ancient Greeks until as late as the 19th century.

**THE WORD 'LEECH'** comes from the Old English *laece*, which is related to *lacnian*, 'to heal'. At one time it was applied not only to the bloodsucking annelids, but also to the doctors who prescribed their use. advised shaving the skin before the leech was applied, adding the reassurance that 'if the leech is hungry it will soon bite'. In case of adherence problems it suggested one should '…roll the leech into a little porter [ale], or moisten the surface with a little blood, or milk, or sugar, or water'. If leeches were to be applied to the gums it warned that a 'leech glass' should be used to keep them in place, otherwise they 'are apt to creep down the patient's throat'.

The use of leeches declined in the 19th century, but surgeons are again making use of the leech's remarkable physiology today. As it sucks blood a leech not only produces an anticoagulant, which prevents clotting, but also a mild anaesthetic, which makes its actions painless. What is more, the leech's gut is home to a bacterium that not only aids the digestion of blood but produces an antibiotic that helps to prevent secondary infection.

# To drive out illness

**All manner of animal products were used in the past to dispel disease. And to keep evil witches at bay – and give protection against the illnesses they caused to humans and livestock – animal parts were sealed inside glass bottles and buried.**

Fat, flesh and blood, as well as the ground hoofs and horns of animals and birds – including the ox, ass, goat, deer, lion, mouse, bat, frog, lizard, snake, swallow, duck and goose – were common 'medicines' in the Egyptian armoury against disease of both humans and domestic animals. Many of these are mentioned specifically in the Ebers papyrus, which dates from around 1500 BC, and is the oldest preserved medical document still in existence.

The aim of the 'witch bottle' was to lure the disease or other harm aimed at you into the bottle, where it could be safely confined. To be most effective it needed to contain material from the person or animal thought to be under threat. This could be blood, hair, nail parings or urine. One such bottle, containing mostly cow fat, was unearthed in Dorset in 2005. It is thought to date from the mid-1700s, when outbreaks of cattle distemper are known to have rampaged through local herds.

**The ancients** believed greatly in the process of fumigation in driving out the demons that caused disease. Animal parts would also be swallowed or the body smeared with mixtures such as the dung of a swallow or goose mixed with the hair of an ass.

# Maggot clinic

**Eating away illness – quite literally – is the medical role of the maggot, in an old technique that is now coming back into use. But maggots need to be carefully chosen and handled to prevent them from causing more problems than they cure.**

Maggots have been known for their healing powers since the 16th century, but maggot therapy began in earnest following the American Civil War and World War I, when battlefield medics noticed that soldiers' wounds that were infested with maggots healed better than those where no maggots were present.

**ALTHOUGH PAIN-FREE,** maggot treatment does not look pleasant, and it can also cause almost unbearable tickling.

The larvae of blowflies, maggots are now used to treat ulcers and other 'flesh-eating' conditions to prevent them from becoming gangrenous. Such treatment is particularly useful for patients who are allergic or resistant to antibiotics. As the maggots devour the infected tissue they clean the skin, preventing the growth of potentially fatal infection. Once the maggots have done their job – by which time they may have increased up to ten times in size – the doctor simply flushes them out.

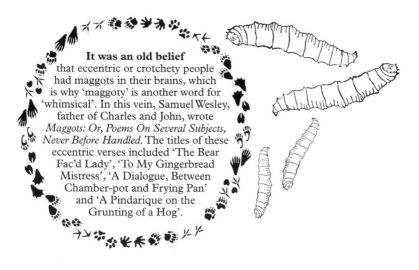

**It was an old belief** that eccentric or crotchety people had maggots in their brains, which is why 'maggoty' is another word for 'whimsical'. In this vein, Samuel Wesley, father of Charles and John, wrote *Maggots: Or, Poems On Several Subjects, Never Before Handled*. The titles of these eccentric verses included 'The Bear Fac'd Lady', 'To My Gingerbread Mistress', 'A Dialogue, Between Chamber-pot and Frying Pan' and 'A Pindarique on the Grunting of a Hog'.

# Just a flea bite?

**Proverbially something hardly worth bothering with, flea bites can certainly be irritating. Today we are lucky that fleas no longer carry the dreaded plague but they are still responsible for spreading typhus, a disease which can be life-threatening.**

Between 1348 and 1357 the bubonic plague, known as the Black Death, wiped out at least a quarter of the population of Europe. 'It is impossible to believe the number who have died,' wrote a French monk, adding:

**THE PARASITICAL LIFESTYLE** of fleas is celebrated in rhyme: 'Great fleas have little fleas/Upon their backs to bite 'em/Little fleas have lesser fleas/And so ad infinitum.'

'Travellers, merchants, pilgrims declare that they have found
cattle wandering without herdsman in fields, towns and
wastelands.'

The plague was not a new disease, having certainly
struck the Athenians in 430 BC, during the Peloponnesian
War, but what neither the ancients nor the medieval citizens
knew was that this dread contagion was spread by the bites
of fleas, which had, in turn, feasted on the blood of infected
black rats. Fleas also carry typhus, another potentially
deadly disease.

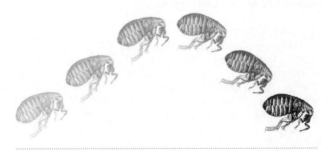

# Mosquitoes – the flying foe

**As notorious as the flea for its ability to spread disease, the mosquito is a potentially deadly pest when it passes on malaria or yellow fever. These two diseases have, between them, killed more people than all the wars in history.**

It is the female mosquito that packs the fatal punch. As she punctures human skin with her long proboscis she may inject, at the same time, the larval forms of a parasite or a virulent virus. The pairings are specific. The malaria parasite *Plasmodium* is carried by the *Anopheles* mosquito, the yellow fever virus by *Aedes aegypti*. Evening is the time when humans are most vulnerable to attack, because, as one medical wit has put it, the mosquito, like other sinners, 'prefers the night hours for its revels'.

The way to stop a mosquito biting you is, it's said, to hold your breath when the insect alights on you. More practical methods include driving them away with clouds of smoke from a fire or protecting oneself with a mosquito net – or destroying the habitats where they breed. Among the places where the latter has been achieved are the notorious lands astride the Panama Canal. During Ferdinand

**The Mosquito Coast** or Mosquitia region lies on the east coast of Nicaragua and Honduras. The name, used by Paul Theroux for his 1981 novel, is derived from the Miskito, the indigenous inhabitants. The hordes of biting insects found in their territory were reputedly able to kill a man in a single night.

de Lesseps' attempt to create this waterway in the 1880s thousands of workers died from malaria and yellow fever, causing the French diplomat and engineer to abandon his dream. The swamps were drained and filled, and the canal was eventually completed by the USA in 1914.

# To ease the rheumatism

**Even our Neanderthal ancestors who lived some 50,000 years ago suffered from the pain of rheumatism and arthritis, which the ancient Egyptians called 'hardening in the limbs'.**

An eelskin or snakeskin garter was once a popular anti-rheumatism accessory. The former were traditionally made in places such as the Fens of eastern England by a very complex method. First, eels were caught in the spring and their heads and tails cut off.
The skins were left to dry in

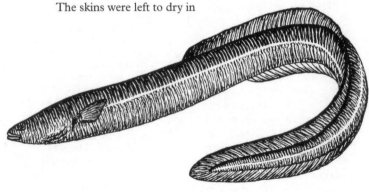

the sun, then softened with fat and stuffed with thyme and lavender. Over the summer they were buried in peat, between layers of mint, so that by the autumn, when damp and cold exacerbated aching joints, they were ready for wear. They were placed just above the knee, by men on the right leg and by women on the left.

## ANTIDOTES TO ACHES
Some more old-fashioned rheumatism remedies featuring animals or animal products, some of which are not for the sensitive or faint hearted:
- Carry a hare's foot in your pocket.
- Hang a piece of dried dog's tongue around your neck.
- Take a cat to bed with you.
- Rub the painful parts with skunk oil.

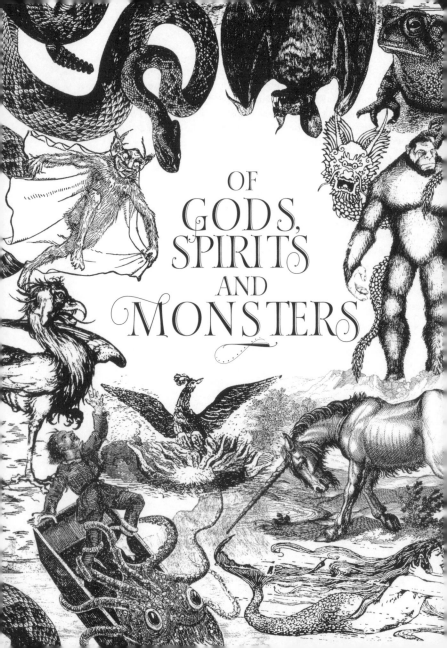

OF
GODS,
SPIRITS
AND
MONSTERS

From the phoenix that arises from the ashes, to Pegasus, the magical winged horse, and from mermaids who lure sailors to their doom to evil serpents, stories abound worldwide of mythical creatures with extraordinary powers. While many of these have obvious connections with living animals and birds, others are almost certainly figments of human imagination – although no less fascinating for that, as the continued search for the Loch Ness Monster undoubtedly proves. And perhaps we should all beware of attacks by such infamous animals as the boggart and bug-a-boo.

That these extraordinary creatures often lurk in the sea is an undoubted indication of the ocean's many dangers. Yet other animal stories relate to bad weather or to the once inexplicable forces responsible for creating earthquakes and volcanic erpuions. Meanwhile in the hostile terrain of the mountains roam elusive creatures such as Bigfoot, also dubbed the Yeti or Abominable Snowman. Some animals are even thought to be people in disguise. These include werewolves, humans able to turn themselves at will into ravening wild animals, and vampires which, in bat form, are the personifications of the living dead.

Not all these creatures are malign by any means. The unicorn, for example, was a creature believed to love purity, while some dragons of Eastern culture have the power to make good triumph over evil. Not only do they symbolize authority, but they were also the bringers of abundance and fertility.

# The mystery of mermaids

**Many legends tell of creatures – half woman, half fish – that inhabit the seas and are able to predict storms. It is widely believed to be unlucky to see one, and even worse to kill one. Grasping the belt or cap of a mermaid will, it is said, give a mortal power over her.**

Mermaids, by repute, live beneath the sea in a land of riches and splendour. From here they lure seafarers to their deaths, then gather up the souls of the dead and keep them in cages. 'The Mermaid', one of a collection of traditional songs assembled by Francis James Child in the 19th century, relates how:

> *'Twas Friday morn when we set sail,*
> *And we had not got far from land,*
> *When the Captain, he spied a lovely mermaid,*
> *With a comb and a glass in her hand.*

In the final verse the ballad tells of the disaster that befalls following the sighting:

*Then three times 'round went our gallant ship,*
*And three times'round went she,*
*And the third time that she went 'round'*
*She sank to the bottom of the sea.*

In Hans Christian Andersen's tale, 'The Little Mermaid', the sea creature falls in love with a prince in a passing ship. In order to be with him, she asks a sea witch to give her human form but has to pay for it with her tongue and is doomed to perpetual silence. Although she waits on him assiduously, he marries a 'true' human. Her heart is broken. Later, she is given the chance to regain her mermaid's tail by killing the prince, but she kills herself instead and joins the 'daughters of the air', spirits destined to wait 300 years for immortality.

**'True life' mermaids** are probably dugongs or manatees, rare marine mammals with heads that somewhat resemble humans in profile and fish-shaped tails. While suckling their single young the females cradle the babies to their breasts with one flipper, in the manner of human mothers.

**IN IRISH LORE**, mermaids are called merrows. They are old pagan women who foretell bad weather, banished from the earth by St Patrick. It is said that the coastal region of Machaire is inhabited by people descended from the union of a man and a mermaid.

# Phoenix rising

**The ancient symbol of the sun (which reappeared each morning) and later of the Resurrection, the phoenix is a bird whose legend has been hugely embellished over the centuries.**

**The phoenix** was the badge of Jane Seymour, the beloved third wife of Henry VIII. It was also a favourite device of Elizabeth I because it symbolized sacrifice and renewal.

According to a well-known version of its myth, the phoenix, said to live for 500 years, is a male bird with beautiful plumage that lives in Arabia. At the end of its life cycle it builds itself a nest of cassia and frankincense twigs, on which it sits to sing a song of rare beauty. The nest is then set on fire by the sun's rays. Both nest and bird burn fiercely and are reduced to ashes. Out of the ashes of the dead phoenix crawls a worm, and from this a new, young phoenix arises. This new phoenix embalms the ashes of the old one in an egg made of myrrh, which it takes to Heliopolis (the

Egyptian city of the sun) where it buries the parent bird in the temple before returning to Arabia.

The Roman naturalist Pliny described the phoenix as being '... as big as an eagle, in colour yellow, and bright as gold, namely all about the neck, the rest of the body a deep red purple; the tail azure blue, intermingled with feathers among of rose carnation colour...'

A Persian creature similar to the phoenix is the fabulous Simurg. According to one legend it lives for up to 1,700 years, and when the young bird hatches, the parent of the opposite sex burns itself to death.

**THE PHOENIX LEGEND** may have arisen from the vulture's habit of taking and flying off with burning pieces of flesh from funeral pyres.

# Hideous winged monsters

**Among the most fearsome creatures of mythology are those with bird-like wings, including the ghastly Harpies and the Gorgons. Their evil powers, especially their calls, were able to wreck the lives of the humans.**

The Harpies were monsters with the heads of women but the claws and wings of eagles or vultures, and were loathsome to behold. Personifications of the storm winds, they were robbers, who carried people off to be tormented in the underworld. Their names forcefully reflect the strength

The word 'harpy' is now used for a greedy, predatory woman, while a gorgon is a woman renowned for the strength of her temper.

 **THE HEAD** of the Medusa is an ancient icon used on shields and breastplates to protect warriors against slaughter.

of their malign influence: Aello means 'storm'; Celeno 'blackness' and Ocypete 'rapid'. They were portrayed on Greek monuments as symbols of death.

Notorious for their hair of living serpents, the three hideous Gorgons were endowed with golden wings and bronze claws. Just one look from them could turn an unfortunate human to stone. The Greek poet Hesiod includes in their number the queen Medusa, the only mortal of the trio. In legend, Medusa met her end when her head was struck off by the hero Perseus, who avoided lethal gaze by using the polished shield of Athene as a mirror to look at her as he wielded his sword. Afterwards, Athene set the head with its writhing snakes in the centre of her shield.

# The elusive sea serpents

Although their existence – and their identity – is disputed, sightings of sea serpents have been regularly reported since ancient times, and they have been held responsible for the fatal wrecking of ships.

'Among fishermen with long experience,' said Aristotle, 'some claim to have seen in the sea animals like beams of wood, black, round and the same thickness throughout.' To others they appeared to have flowing manes like horses; yet others noticed long heads and scaly skins like those of crocodiles.

One vivid report of an undulating, snake-like creature seen off Gloucester Bay, Massachusetts in 1817 reads: 'We counted twenty bunches

No creature consistent with descriptions of a sea serpent has ever been washed ashore. Decaying remains of basking sharks have been put forward as possibilities, but the mystery remains. Perhaps, some speculate, this is because the sea serpent confines itself to deep water. Whether it is a relation of the giant squid (or the Kraken) or an eel, shark or turtle, is yet to be determined.

[humps]… His head was of a dark brown colour, formed like a seal's and shined with a glossy appearance…his head was large as a barrel for we could see it when he was about four miles from us.'

As well as more than 400 seemingly bona fide sightings there have been many hoaxes. These include the 1871 description of a beast with '…an enormous fan-shaped tail… overlapping scales [which]…open and shut with every arch of his sinuous back coloured like a rainbow…'

**SEA SERPENT TRAITS**

Features consistently reported down the years include:
- Many small humps along the back.
- Several big coils visible above the water.
- A mane on the neck.
- Prominent eyes.
- A long neck and small head.
- Many fins.

# Norway's own Kraken

On hot days, so Norwegian sailors of the 16th century reported, the sea would turn murky and the monstrous Kraken would emerge. When it sank again it created a great whirlpool that had the power to pull even the largest ship to its doom.

The bonus of this risky situation for the fishermen was that the appearance of the Kraken coincided with an abundance of fish. What also happened was that the sea suddenly decreased in depth – a signal they took to mean that the animal was about to surface. This recalls the phenomenon of the 'deep scattering layer' of myriad small squid, which causes echo-sounders to give false readings. And the Kraken itself was almost certainly a giant squid.

**In his 1953 sci-fi novel** *The Kraken Wakes*, John Wyndham tells the story of a world in which the seas are occupied by a foreign life form that has arrived from outer space in an attempt to take over the earth. Its American title was *Out of the Deeps*.

First described by Erik Pontoppidan in his 1752 *History of Norway*, the Kraken lives on in Norwegian legend. A bishop was even said to have celebrated a mass on its back, taking it to be an island. In his *Juvenilia*, published when he was 21, Tennyson included a poem dedicated to this sea monster:

> *Below the thunders of the upper deep,*
> *Far, far beneath the abysmal sea,*
> *His ancient, dreamless, uninvaded sleep*
> *The Kraken sleepeth: faintest sunlights flee*

*About his shadowy sides; above him swell*
*Huge sponges of millennial growth and height;*
*And far away into the sickly light,*
*From many a wondrous grot and secret cell*
*Unnumber'd and enormous polypi*
*Winnow with giant arms the slumbering green.*
*There he hath lain for ages, and will lie*
*Battening upon huge sea-worms in his sleep,*
*Until the latter fire shall heat the deep;*
*Then once by man and angels to be seen,*
*In roaring he shall rise and on the surface die.*

# The monster of the loch

Most famed of all the unidentified water dwellers is
Scotland's Loch Ness Monster. The subject of media hype
and hoaxes, as well as serious scientific investigation,
'Nessie's' true identity remains a mystery.

Reports of a creature in Loch Ness
go back at least 1,500 years. St
Adomnan's medieval *Life of St
Columba* tells how, in 565 AD,
Columba, by raising his voice
to the creature, saved the
life of a Pict who was being
attacked by it in the river
Ness. On 2 May 1933, the
*Inverness Courier* (whose
editor dubbed the creature
'a monster') ran the story
of Mr and Mrs John Mackay,
who had seen 'an enormous
animal rolling and plunging' on
the surface of Loch Ness. In the
media frenzy that ensued, a circus offered
a reward of £20,000 for the monster's capture.

**Various theories** have
been proposed for the
monster's identity. These include
a prehistoric plesiosaur and the
species of sturgeon that has been
found in streams close to Loch
Ness. Another theory is that the
'humps' are in fact disruptions
of the water caused by minor
volcanic activity at the
bottom of the loch.

Reports of Nessie have continued to flow ever since this
incident. In March 1994, however, it came to light that one
Marmaduke Wetherall had faked the famous photograph of
a long-necked creature that was attributed to surgeon RK
Wilson in 1934. In another hoax, the ornithologist Sir Peter
Scott gave the creature the name *Nessiteras rhombopteryx* after
seeing a blurred underwater photograph taken in the early
1970s by group led by the American lawyer Robert Rines.
The name is an anagram of 'monster hoax by Sir Peter S'.

## THE CULT OF NESSIE

The Loch Ness Monster has appeared in many fictional – often bizarre – contexts.

**Dr Who** – in the 1975 series, it is an alien cyborg controlled by extraterrestrial Zygons.

**The Simpsons** – in episode 224, 'Monty Can't Buy Me Love', Mr Burns, Homer and others drain the loch, capture the monster and take it back to the USA. Mr Burns gives it a job in a casino.

**Freddie as FR**07 – Jon Acevski's 1992 animated parody of the Bond films, in which Scottie the monster befriends an enchanted frog prince, and together they defeat an enemy wreaking revenge on the world by shrinking landmarks all over London.

**The Private Life of Sherlock Holmes** – Billy Wilder's 1970 classic in which Holmes encounters the monster while investigating a secret society whose members are developing a submarine in the loch.

**Nessie and Me** – in Jim Wynorski's 2016 film a 9-year-old boy moves to a house beside the loch and hears of the monster which subsequently plays a part in a saving the town from a ruthless businessman.

# Follow the footprints

**Some of the world's most elusive creatures – if they exist at all – are known only from the footprints they are alleged to leave. These have given rise to legends such as those of Bigfoot and the Jersey Devil.**

Bigfoot, a huge ape-like creature believed to tramp across various parts of north-western USA and western Canada, was 'discovered' in 1811 by the British explorer David Thompson. Its footprints have supposedly been measured at 2ft (60cm) long and 8in (20cm) wide. Despite a convincing film made in 1967, its existence is yet to be confirmed.

The Yeti, also dubbed 'the Abominable Snowman', roams (if it does exist) the Himalayas where, to the Nepalese, it is significant as a spiritual rather than an actual physical entity. Said to be ape-like, 10ft (3m) tall, with feet twice the size of a man's, its footprints are believed to range over vast tracts of open snow. In reality, these may well be the prints of human boots enlarged by the melting of the snow.

In 1735, a Mrs Leeds in New Jersey was said to have given birth to a cursed child (her 13th) with a horse's head and hooves, wings and a snake's tail. During the 19th century this

**The Chupacarbra,** an alleged predator of South America whose name is Spanish for 'goat sucker', is said to drink the blood of various farm animals, leaving their corpses in the fields with incision wounds on their necks. Some people claim to have seen the creature in remote areas, and it is often described as having 'spines' down its back.

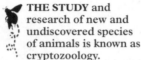

**THE STUDY** and research of new and undiscovered species of animals is known as cryptozoology.

being was seen from time to time, but over a five-day period in January 1909 over 100 people reported sightings. As well as hoof prints in the snow, there were accounts of the Jersey Devil flying overs towns and attacking domestic animals.

# Tales of the thunderbird

**By flapping its wings it caused thunderclaps to roar. As it blinked, lightning flashed in the sky. So runs the story of the gigantic thunderbird of North American Indian folklore.**

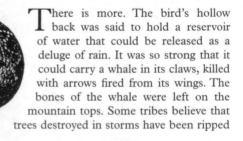

There is more. The bird's hollow back was said to hold a reservoir of water that could be released as a deluge of rain. It was so strong that it could carry a whale in its claws, killed with arrows fired from its wings. The bones of the whale were left on the mountain tops. Some tribes believe that trees destroyed in storms have been ripped

**IN SOME AMERICAN TALES,** thunder is the rattle of a black rattlesnake, which carries a supernatural creature on its back. For others it is the sound of a great bat's wing.

open by the thunderbird's claws to extract the huge grubs that are its favourite food.

As well as influencing the weather, in the mythology of Plains and Woodlands Indians the thunderbird wages constant warfare with underwater creatures, especially horned snakes. Northwest Indians, who depict the thunderbird on their tepees, are among those for whom the images are a means of warding off the attentions of evil spirits.

***Thunderbirds,*** first aired in 1965, was a children's action-adventure TV show set in the 2020s. Made by Sylvia and Gerry Anderson, it used a new form of puppetry they called 'Supermarionation'. The show's title came from a letter written to his family by Gerry Anderson's older brother during World War II, while he was serving on an American airbase called 'Thunderbird Field'.

# Curses of the 'were' creatures

**Werewolves – humans able to turn themselves at will into ravening wild animals – have been feared since real wolves roamed at large among our ancestors' habitations. These embodiments of evil are based on the concept of 'the beast within'.**

Influenced by the mysterious process known as lycanthropy, witches, sorcerers, and others with evil powers were believed able to turn themselves into wolves. (The term 'werewolf' comes from the Old English *wer*, meaning man.) The 19th-century author Emma Phipson vividly conjures

**IN THE 2005 MOVIE** hit from animator Nick Park, Wallace and Gromit go on the trail of a were-rabbit, which is eating prize-winning vegetables.

their menace: 'Human beings when under this delusion,' she says, 'roamed through forests and desert places actuated by the same passions as the wild beasts whose name they bore. They howled, walked on all fours, tore up graves in search of prey, attacked unarmed passengers, devoured children, and committed the wildest excesses.'

Where fear of werewolves took hold it could cause panic across entire communities. It is reported that in 1600, in the Jura mountains between France and Switzerland, lycanthropy was so rife that men and women gathered themselves into packs and roamed the country. And in France, the *loup-garou* is still an object of terror. No weapon is effective against a werewolf unless, some believe, it has been blessed in a chapel dedicated to St Hubert, the patron saint of hunters.

Apart from wolves, other 'were' creatures are known in various parts of the world. In South America, for instance, there is a lasting belief in were-jaguars.

The concept of the werewolf resonates strongly in legends surrounding Lycaon, the mythical ruler of Arcadia. In the most common, related by Ovid, Lycaon was turned into a wolf because he angered Zeus by serving him a 'hash of human flesh' when the god visited Lycaon's court in the guise of a simple traveller; this was a child sacrifice, possibly of Lycaon's own son. This gave rise to the story that a man was turned into a wolf at each annual sacrifice to Zeus, but recovered his human form if he abstained from devouring human flesh for ten years.

# Tales of the vampire

Although anyone who sucks blood can be dubbed a vampire, in the natural world it is vampire bats that have the most bloodthirsty reputation. But most fearsome are the 'living dead' – the vampires who, often in bat form, attack unwary innocents.

Of all supernatural monsters the vampire is among the best known. Traditionally, his eyes gleam red, his breath is foul, his fingernails pointed and he has hairs on the palms of his hands. Some are said to have only a single nostril. Returning from the grave, complete with bats' wings, the vampire is said to turn his victim into yet another such horror with his bite.

The idea of the vampire existed in legend long before Bram Stoker crystallized it into Dracula, taking the monster's name from *dracul*, the Romanian word for 'devil'. Where vampire activity was believed to be rife, it was customary to take a white stallion that had never been to stud – and never stumbled – into a graveyard. Any graves that the horse refused to walk over were those of vampires.

**The American Stroke Association** has reported the success of a drug made from the saliva of the vampire bat in busting the clots that lodge in the brain and cause strokes.

**AGAINST A VAMPIRE**

To defend yourself against a vampire it is said that you should:

- Wear a silver amulet, or carry any silver object in your pocket.
- Wear garlic flowers around your neck or place them in the window – vampires hate their smell.
- Carry or wear a crucifix – the symbol of Christ will neutralize the evil.
- Drive a stake through its heart.
- Shoot it with a silver bullet, ideally made from a crucifix that has been melted down.

# The croak of the evil toad

Toads are feared as witches or evil men in animal form, although 'toad-magic' is also an old means of destroying witches' powers.

**At the trial** of the Bury St Edmunds witches in 1665, a Dr Jacob declared that he had found a toad in the bed of a child named Amy Duny. After he had thrown the creature in the fire, Amy developed burns on her arms – a sure sign to those in authority of a witch acting in disguise.

The natural reaction of a toad, when alarmed, to exude various poisonous irritants is undoubtedly significant to its links with witchcraft.

Toadmen, able to make the most unruly horse stand still, were recorded in England. To acquire such powers a man had to skin a toad or peg it to an anthill until the insects had stripped its bones clean. He then had to carry the bones in his pocket until they were dry and, at midnight under a full moon, float them on a stream. The bones would screech and one would detach itself and head upstream. Catching this 'rogue' bone bestowed a toadman's powers.

## ANTI-WITCH TREATMENT
Toads were once used in this charm intended to rob a witch of her evil attributes, and prevent her from influencing your life:
1 Take three small-necked jars.
2 Place in each a toad's heart studded with thorns and a frog's liver into which new pins have been inserted.
3 Cork the jars and bury them in three different churchyards, 7in (17.5cm) below the surface and 7ft (2.1m) from the church porch.
4 During each burial, say the Lord's Prayer backwards.

# The serpent god

Known throughout Middle America, the serpent god Quetzalcoatl (whose name means 'green feather snake') was originally the god of the air and wind but was also a divine creator and the ruler of the ancient Toltec people.

Quetzalcoatl is, at once, heaven and earth, light and darkness, life and death. As a creator god he travelled to Mictlan, the underworld, retrieved some bones and sprinkled them with his blood, bringing human life into being. He was also a teacher, showing people how to farm and weave cotton and also how to make calendars and interpret the movements of the stars. All over Mesoamerica, Quetzalcoatl was considered to be the god of the morning star, while his twin brother Xoloti was the evening star. He was believed to have created the present world by visiting the underworld where he created humankind.

THE PLUMES on the head of Quetzalcoatl are those of the quetzal bird, a creature still celebrated in Mexican festival dances. Dressed in sumptuous feathered costumes, the dancers, called *quetzales,* perform a set of ritual steps that scholars think is a tribute to the life-giving powers of the sun.

According to Toltec myth, a pale skinned god-king named Quetzalcoatl was sent into exile by the dark god Tezcatlipoca ('smoking mirror'), and crossed the Gulf of Mexico on a raft of snakes, vowing to return. When, in 1591 (considered an auspicious year by the Aztecs, who claimed descent from the Toltecs) the Spanish adventurer Hernán Cortés – a pale-skinned European – arrived on the coast of Mexico he was believed to be the returning god. As a result, the Aztec emperor Montezuma received Cortés graciously, but was captured and killed during the Spanish conquest of the Aztec capital.

**The resplendent quetzal** (*Pharomachrus mocino*) is a spectacular resident of the forests to the east of the Bolivian Andes, its red front contrasting starkly with its metallic green back, white undertail and long shimmering green tail feathers. To the ancient Maya the quetzal symbolized freedom – because a quetzal will die in captivity – and wealth, because the quetzal feathers were, with jade, the Maya traders' most sought-after treasures.

# The unicorn –
# one horned wonder

**Of all legendary beasts, the unicorn is among the most famous and benign. It is also widely regarded as a symbol of purity, and as such is associated with the Virgin Mary who was able to tame it.**

'The fiercest animal,' wrote Pliny, 'is the unicorn, which in the rest of the body resembles a horse, but in the head a stag, in the feet an elephant, and in the tail a boar, and has a deep bellow, and a single black horn three feet long projecting from the middle of the forehead. They say,' he concluded, 'that it is impossible to capture this animal alive.'

Of all its attributes, the unicorn's horn was most endowed with magical and medicinal properties. The horn would also, it was said, purify the water in a well with a single touch, especially if used to trace the sign of the cross. Horns reputed to have such gifts, probably the tusks of narwhal, were prized in the courts of Renaissance Europe. The horn of the unicorn was once used to detect the presence of poison in the food of kings. Just one touch, it was said, was sufficient to reveal a life-threatening ingredient.

As well as the Virgin Mary, other virgins were believed able to tame the lustful unicorn, whose horn symbolized male desire. The Holy Hunt for the unicorn, in which a beautiful naked virgin had to be tied to a tree in order to attract the beast, became an allegory in which Christ is the unicorn who is attracted by the Virgin Mary and killed to save the world's sinners.

## THE LION AND THE UNICORN
The contest between these two great beasts is thought to symbolize the triumph of summer over spring, and can be traced back to at least 3500 BC. However this early 18th-century nursery rhyme probably refers to the amalgamation of the arms of Scotland and those of England in 1603:

*The lion and the unicorn*
*Were fighting for the crown;*
*The lion beat the unicorn*
*All around the town.*

*Some gave them white bread,*
*And some gave them brown;*
*Some gave them plum cake*
*And drummed them out of town.*

# 'Here be dragons'

**... Or so it was written on outlines of remote parts of the world by early mapmakers. Dragons bad and good feature in myth and legend all over the world.**

With the head and horns of a ram, a lion's forelimbs, a scaly reptilian body (like that of a crocodile) and an eagle's claws, the dragon depicted in white glaze on the Ishtar Gate in ancient Babylon is one of the oldest known renditions of this mythical creature. From it evolved the familiar fearsome animal with sharp talons, forked tongue, glaring eyes (often glowing with a red reflection from the treasures it guarded), flared nostrils breathing fire capable of destroying anything in its path – even entire countries – and a thunderous voice.

**As a symbol** of power, the dragon was adopted by the Romans as an icon on their standard, and it is the association with invading Romans that is thought to have led King Henry VII, who was of Welsh descent, to use it on his coat of arms.

Dragons of old were so omnipotent that they could control not only the weather – bringing about eclipses by swallowing the sun or moon – but also the destiny of humankind. In many cultures men were thought to become dragons after their death, and there was also a belief that after death the souls of the wicked would be left to the mercy of a fire-breathing dragon. When the dead were buried with their earthly treasures, it was dragons who guarded this bounty. Another belief was that, if planted, dragons' teeth would grow into an army of men.

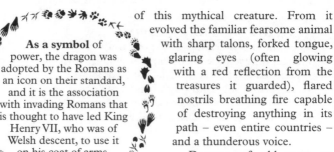

The Greek word *drakos*, meaning 'eye', is the root of the dragon's name, and ties in with the idea that the dragon is a guardian of treasure. In the Christian tradition,

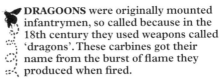

**DRAGOONS** were originally mounted infantrymen, so called because in the 18th century they used weapons called 'dragons'. These carbines got their name from the burst of flame they produced when fired.

however, it is often interchangeable with the serpent. So in Revelation, in St Michael's battle, 'the great dragon was thrown down, that ancient serpent that was called the Devil…'

---

**DRAGON LANGUAGE**

Many current words and phrases maintain a link with the mythological beast, including:

**To chase the dragon** – to smoke opium or heroin. The fumes produced look like dragons' breath.

**Flying dragon** – a colloquial term for a meteor.

**To sow dragon's teeth** – to do something intended to quell strife, but which in fact foments it even more.

**Dragon's blood** – a reddish-brown resin with a spicy fragrance extracted from palms such as *Calamus draco*. Jilted lovers traditionally throw it on the fire and chant a rhyme in order to restore their broken dreams.

**Dragon's teeth** – anti-tank obstacles used in World War II.

---

# Enter the dragon

❧

**Essentially benign, unlike their western counterparts, the dragons of the East were believed to control different aspects of the world. Their ancient powers are remembered in the dragon dances that still take place at Chinese New Year.**

Wang Fu, a Chinese philosopher of the Han Dynasty (206 BC – 220 AD) painted a vivid portrait of the eastern dragon. It had a complex make up – a camel's head with stag's horns, an elephant's tusks, demon's eyes and cow's ears. Its triple-jointed body, ending in a serpent's tail, had a clam's belly, a carp's scales, an eagle's claws and the feet of a tiger. Of the creature's 117 scales, he said, 81 are imbued with yang, and 36 with yin, making its good influences outweigh the bad, and ensuring that it is essentially male, rather than female.

To the ancients, the most important role of eastern dragons was their control of water, either in rivers, seas, lakes and wells, or as rain

**TO THE JAPANESE**, dragons are by no means totally benign. Some are believed to demand the annual sacrifice of a virgin. The Dragon King of Japanese legend dwells beneath the ocean protected by a retinue of sea serpents, fishes and sea monsters.

falling from the clouds. When angry they created storms, thunder and lightning but they could also bring about droughts by gathering up all the waters of a region into baskets. Because water was an essential life-giving element, the dragon was a symbol of fertility.

**The dragon** symbolized imperial authority, and was held in highest esteem during the Qing Dynasty (1644–1912). Everything used by the emperor was given a dragon epithet – he slept on a dragon bed, was rowed in a dragon boat and sat on the dragon throne. When he died, it was said, 'The dragon has ascended to heaven.'

# The ghastly griffin

**Also known as the griffon, gryphon or gryps, the griffin, like the dragon, is a mythological guardian of treasure. This winged creature has also been long employed as a protective emblem.**

The griffin has the body of a lion and the head and wings of an eagle. Pliny, in his *Natural History*, writes of the struggle between the

WHILE FEMALE GRIFFINS were winged, the males were armed with spikes in place of wings. A variant of the griffin was the hyppogriff, which had a horse's body and an eagle's wings.

griffins and the Arimaspi, 'a people noted for having one eye in the middle of their forehead'. There was, he records, '...a continual battle between the Arimaspi and griffins in the vicinity of the latter's mines. The griffin,' he continues, 'is a type of wild beast with wings, as is commonly reported,

**The griffin** is depicted on Minoan palaces on the island of Crete, where it is thought to act as a protective device. Much used in heraldry, since the 16th century it has been the badge of Grays Inn, one of the four Inns of Court in London that admit students wishing to become barristers.

which digs gold out of tunnels. The griffins guard the gold and the Arimaspi try to seize it, each with remarkable greed.'

Griffins were renowned in Greek mythology for being the enemies of horses. They were also reputed to be responsible for pulling either the chariot of the sun across the sky each day or the chariot of the goddess Nemesis, the avenger of wrongdoing.

# Magical horses

Many gods and goddesses are credited with taking on the forms of horses, animals long revered for their strength and usefulness. And horses are believed, in many traditions, to help pull the sun across the sky.

Magical transformations are the stuff of mythology. To avoid the advances of Poseidon, the Greek sea god, the goddess Demeter transformed herself into a mare. But her efforts were in vain, for he turned himself into a stallion and as a result of their union they became parents to the magical winged black horse Arion. It was Arion who was later borrowed by Hercules in his labours.

**THE WINGED PEGASUS** is the logo of the Mobil corporation and of the Reader's Digest.

Most divine of all the mythical horses was Pegasus, believed to have been created from the blood shed from the snake-headed Medusa after her head was severed by Perseus. Tamed by Bellerophon, with the help of a bridle given to him by the goddess Athene, Pegasus helped the hero defeat the Chimera. But later, when Bellerophon tried to ride the horse up to the top of Mount Olympus – in order to reach heaven – Pegasus threw his rider off. Pegasus was then commandeered by Zeus to fetch and carry the thunderbolts with which he attacked earth's mortal inhabitants.

**One day,** so legend relates, the Muses were singing and playing on Mount Helicon but were making so much noise that Poseidon sent Pegasus to quell their merriment. On arriving at the top of the mountain, Pegasus had only to paw the ground to quell the noise. From his footprint sprang the Hippocrene fountain, the source of poetic inspiration.

# The sacred bull giant

**Nowhere in the ancient world was the bull more sacred than on the island of Crete, where the legend of the Minotaur arose. With a man's body and a bull's head, this giant creature fed on human flesh.**

**THE MINOTAUR was used as a symbol on the standard of one of the Roman legions.**

In ancient Crete, goes the story, Pasiphaë, wife of King Minos of Crete, fell in love with a white bull, which appeared from the sea as a sign from Poseidon (ruler of the oceans) of Minos's sovereignty. To seduce the creature she hid herself inside a hollow wooden cow, covered with hide, which had been made for her by the cunning craftsman Daedalus. Together they wheeled it into the pasture where the bull was kept – and so the Minotaur was conceived and born.

To conceal his shame, Minos kept the Minotaur in a labyrinth at Knossos – which was also designed and made by Daedalus. Here the cannibalistic beast was regularly fed on the bodies of seven maidens and seven youths, all brought as tribute from Athens, which Minos had previously defeated in war, and left to wander the labyrinth's paths unaware of their fate. Present for the third of these 'sacrifice sessions' was Theseus, the son of King Aegeus of Athens, who planned to kill the creature with the help of Minos's daughter Ariadne. To prevent Theseus getting lost as he retraced his path through the maze, Ariadne gave him a skein of thread to mark his route, as well as the sword with which he performed his heroic feat.

**The bull** was the Cretan symbol of fertility – its strength and sexuality were believed to be concentrated in its horns.

# The mighty wolf

Universally revered – and feared – the wolf takes on massive form and monstrous powers in ancient tales, especially those of Scandinavia. The Fenris Wolf even had the earth's destiny in its sights.

A huge monster in the form of a wolf, Fenris (or Fenrir) was not only strong but invulnerable. The gape of his jaws was so large that it reached between earth and heaven. Warned by an oracle that the Fenris Wolf, together with the Midgard Serpent, would be instrumental in the destruction of the earth, the gods decided that it must be kept under control. Since it quickly snapped every 'normal' rope used to tie it up, it was to be kept instead on a cord made by dwarfs and composed of six 'impossible' threads: the noise of a cat's footfall, the beards of women, the roots of a mountain, the sensibilities of a bear, the breath of fish, and the spittle of birds.

**AT RAGNARÔK**, the twilight of the gods, the wolf will break free of his chains, join in battle against the gods and devour the great ruler Odin and with him the sun.

This confinement was not achieved without incident. Suspicious of what was to happen, the wolf insisted that if he was to be tied up, one of the gods would first have to put his hand in the animal's mouth. Only Tyr, the god of war, dared to do so – and lost a hand in the process – but the creature was successfully bound to a rock, called Gioll, with a sword clamped between his teeth to prevent him from biting.

ROMULUS AND REMUS

# Beware the boggart and bug-a-boo

**There are many good reasons for children to behave, not least the fear of weird animals (with weirder names) or little people with animal features that are coming to terrorize them.**

The boggart, a type of Celtic hobgoblin, is a mischievous creature that often has fur, a tail or other animal accoutrements. Badly behaved children, especially in Yorkshire and Lancashire, are still threatened with being thrown into the 'boggart hole'. In its most evil form, which can haunt adults as well as children, the boggart – also called a shriker, barguest or trash – is a death omen that appears in the form of a white cow or horse, or sometimes as a black or white dog with massive paw pads, a shaggy coat and glaring eyes the size of saucers. Are boggarts real? In 1825, so one documented account relates, a Manchester tradesman was attacked by a huge headless dog, which put its feet on his shoulders and pushed him all the way home.

The bug-a-boo, also called the bodach or bugbear, will, it's said, kidnap naughty children. It comes down the chimney with no warning. Like the boggart, it probably gets its name from the Middle English word *bogge,* meaning 'terror'. When called bugbears they are thought, literally, to take on the shape of a bear and will actually eat their victims. They are sent, goes the old English proverb, 'to scare babes'.

**Boggarts can be helpful** – they are reputed to assist with everything from housework to reaping and gathering the harvest. But when annoyed they will exert their revenge by making milk and cream curdle and by banging kitchen pots and pans together at night, making so much noise that no one can sleep.

# Mystic water horses

**Among the weird inhabitants of the water are various horse-like creatures with mystical powers. They may also get up to all kinds of mischief.**

The chariot of the Greek sea god Poseidon was pulled by a hippocampus, whose name comes from *hippos*, meaning horse and *kampos*, a sea monster. With a horse's head and upper body, it had hind parts like a fish or dolphin. It was said that as Poseidon rode through the waters the waves would open up ahead of him so that his chariot did not get wet and that sea monsters would swim up from the depths to pay him homage.

By contrast, mischief-making is the penchant of the Kelpie, also known as the water-horse or Nykur. This creature, which had hooves that pointed backward, was reputed to be able to change its shape at will. It was believed to lead men astray by enticing them to ride it across a river, then plunge into the water and drown them. Disaster was most likely to strike if the rider mentioned Christ's name.

Hippocampus is the generic name of the sea horse, an aptly named oddity of the fish world which has a horse-like head and swims upright. It is also peculiar in that the male gives birth to the young. When the fish mate the female lays her eggs in the 'brood pouch' on his belly.

Because it looks rather like a sea horse, there is an area of the brain named the hippocampus. Lying in the 'primitive', unconscious part of the brain the hippocampus is particularly involved with the processing of our memories.

# The charming sirens

**The sweet singing of the Sirens was enough to lure sailors to disaster. These maidens, part human, part bird, were resisted by Odysseus and Jason, two great heroes of mythology.**

When they heard the Sirens' beautiful melodies, sung from rocks off the Italian coast, sailors were doomed, it was said, because they were driven to steer their ships onto the rocks, or to jump into the sea and drown. Or they could be so besotted by the sound of the seductresses that they forgot everything – including food – and starved to death. Consequently their island home was 'piled with boneheaps of men now rotted away'.

So how to resist the Sirens' lure? In his Odyssey, Homer tells how Odysseus was warned by Circe that any man listening to the Sirens, the 'enchanters of all mankind' has no prospect of coming home and 'delighting his wife and little children'. On her advice he ordered his men to stuff their ears with beeswax to prevent them from hearing the music. Odysseus himself was tied to the ship's mast so that despite hearing the Sirens' strains he was powerless to steer or swim to his death, though Circe warned that 'if you supplicate your men and implore them to set you free, then they must tie you fast with even more lashings'.

In the story of Jason and the Argonauts, the hero is saved from the Sirens' lure with the help of Orpheus, whose playing, reputed to be so sweet that it 'charmed the stones and trees to dance or to gather round him' outclassed that of the evil maidens.

# INDEX

**Plant Lore and Legend**
Ruth Binney
ISBN: 978-1-910821-10-7

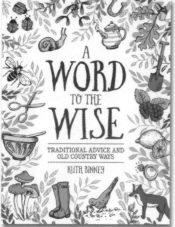

**A Word to the Wise**
Ruth Binney
ISBN: 978-1-910821-11-4

**Amazing and Extraordinary Facts:**
The English Countryside
Ruth Binney
ISBN: 978-1-910821-01-5

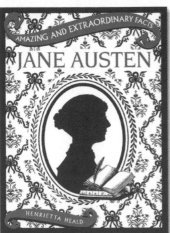

**Amazing and Extraordinary Facts:**
Jane Austen
Henrietta Heald
ISBN: 978-1-910821-12-1

For more great books visit our website at www.rydonpublishing.co.uk

## THE AUTHOR

**Ruth Binney** has been studying nature and the
countryside for over 50 years. She holds a degree
in Natural Sciences from Cambridge University
and has been involved in countless publications
during her career as an editor. She is the author of
many successful natural history and nostalgia titles,
including *Plant Lore and Legend*, *A Word to the Wise*
and *Amazing and Extraordinary Facts: The English
Countryside*. She lives in *Yeovil, Somerset*.
www.ruthbinney.com

## PICTURE CREDITS